BEYOND THE
GRIND

*How To Do Work That Matters, Travel The World
For Free, And Escape The Daily Grind Before
It's Too Late...*

Dave Rogenmoser & Chris Hull

First Printing, 2015

ISBN 13: 978-1-5115-4414-6

Books may be purchased in quantity by contacting the authors, Dave Rogenmoser and Chris Hull by email at team@ getbeyondthegrind.com

To request a speaking engagement, contact the authors at team@getbeyondthegrind.com

www.getbeyondthegrind.com

TABLE OF CONTENTS

Dedicated to our wonderful parents, who gave us dreams to pursue and helped make us the men who could achieve them.

And to our amazing Kickstarter team, who funded this project when it was just an idea. You guys really rock.

INTRODUCTION

We all grow up wanting to do great things, yet life doesn't always seem to deliver on that promise, does it? Most experts agree that your twenties provide the greatest opportunity to change the trajectory of your future - for better or for worse. We all enter this decade dreaming of a life of purpose and freedom with endless opportunities at your fingertips. Yet, the majority of us exit this decade grumbling about being squeezed into the mold society has forced on us. We find ourselves reminiscing on the "best years of our lives" and clinging to the idea of retirement - when we hope to start living fully again.

The world has this sneaky way of selling us all on the daily grind. This book is about helping you escape it. We are going to show you exactly what steps to take to live life Beyond the Grind, and start living a life of freedom, purpose, and passion. This book is for people who don't think climbing the ladder of corporate America is purpose enough. It's for people who are entering the workforce and know they want "more" from their life, even if they aren't sure how to get there or what that exactly means. This book is for people who don't want to be average, but aspire to do great things. It's not for dreamers, it's for doers. And it's written by guys who are doing it now.

As men in the latter-half of our twenties, we offer a

unique perspective. We've lived in multiple states and countries and have backpacked through different parts of the world. We've worked dozens of jobs and even founded multiple early-stage companies. We are absolutely passionate about inspiring people to define what they want out of life and grow into the best version of themselves. Unfortunately, there is a growing disconnect between what people want from their lives and what they ultimately get. That's why this book had to be written.

Students, businessmen, and all folks across all careers who want this life of freedom have already experienced success by implementing the tips and lessons found in this book. Nathan, a student and entrepreneur from Kansas State, says "This book is practical and to the point - it inspired me to start my own business while in college!" We hope this book jumpstarts more Nathans into all sorts of careers and paths.

If you read and apply this book to your life, we promise that you'll know exactly how to take a trip anywhere in the world in the next 45 days using free airline and hotel reward points. We promise you'll start doing work that matters deeply to you. That you will be able to recalibrate the current trajectory of your life and will walk away motivated to do great things. And finally, we promise this isn't one more fluffy, self-help book to put up on the shelf and collect dust. It's a meaty read designed to create change.

Don't be the person who misses out on opportunities in life and settles for normal. Don't be the person who knows deep down that they were created for something more. Be the kind of person other people marvel at. The kind of person other people see and say, "I want my life to look more like theirs." Be the kind of person who takes action and does so immediately.

The powerful ideas and tips you're about to read have created great amounts of change in our own lives and have been proven to create positive, long-lasting results. The next step to living the life you've always dreamed of is in this book. Each chapter will give you new insight as you strive to break out of the daily grind. Take control of your life right now, don't settle for average, and enjoy the new life you're creating.

CHAPTER ONE

ESCAPE FROM THE GRIND

As I drove to the airport to pick up a friend, the gnawing had finally gotten to me. I was a wreck. I picked up the phone and called Chris.

"Hello?"

"Chris, I'm freaking out right now. I can't do this anymore. It's just too hard."

"Whoa, what's going on, Dave?"

"It's too hard, man. I just want to get a normal job with a steady paycheck, and not be an entrepreneur anymore - I don't know if I'm cut out for it."

Welcome to our lives.

Chris and I are entrepreneurs trying to live out our ideals and aspirations. But that's the easy part, right? We are passionately pursuing a life "Beyond the Grind," and in some respects, we're doing a really great job of it. But in a lot of ways, we're just at the beginning of the journey and making lots of mistakes. In writing this book, we made a commitment to be real and honest - even if that made us nervous. We realize we don't have all the answers, but we do have some.

We hear about way too many people who are somewhere along a path they hate. We look around at many of our friends from college, dreading the next 40 years of their life until they can retire and do what they want. They've all been told, "That's just the way life is."

Well, we've been sold a lie. We've been told the above is called "life." College kids are told, "Oh, live it up. Those are the best four years of your life!" But here's our question: Do they have to be? Do I have to have 'the best four years of my life' only 25% of the way in? Does everything have to be downhill from there? Is there a way to have each year of life be better and more fulfilling than the one before? We think there is. And that's exactly the life we're running after.

Chris and I wanted to live and work around some of our best friends from college and focus deeply on building those friendships. So we do. We wanted to live in a cool place with lots of connections to great people. So we moved to the DC area. (Annapolis, actually. Come and visit us!). We wanted to have freedom with our finances and time so we started our own software-based businesses, and then a digital marketing firm with our partner, JP. These are some of the things we want out of life. Do you know what it is that you want? We've taken these first steps, and we'd like to invite you to come with us.

Benefits of Living Beyond The Grind

A while back, my roommate Phil and I were dreaming about going on an international trip. After a twenty minute discussion, we landed on a location. The next day we bought our last-minute plane tickets to Peru, and 8 days later we took off on a three week, INCREDIBLE trip to see Machu Picchu, go dune-bugging, take wine vineyard tours, and make rich memories with a bunch of interesting people we met along the way.

For me, travel is something I really enjoy and I want it to be a big part of my life. This type of trip isn't possible for almost any of my friends, but because I have been designing my life to accommodate things like this, I made it work. I gathered over 200,000 air and hotel miles in the month before the trip, and have plenty left over to spare. (I'll teach you how to do this in chapter 8.)

I still worked on my business via the Starbucks internet while down there. I still stayed connected to the closest people in my life. I came back when I was ready to come home, and life kept right on going.

Beyond The Grind is not just about working harder. I'll be honest - there are a lot of people who work harder than we do. Hard work is a great thing and part of living a fulfilling life. We are going to challenge you to leverage your hard work with strategic thinking, cultivating a new mindset in which problems become opportunities, and working hard on the very few things that provide the majority of the value in your life. Beyond The Grind is about working smart AND hard to achieve the deep purpose and freedom you desire.

* * *

"I think we could definitely have a private jet someday. Why wouldn't we?"

My group of friends looked back at me with blank stares. That was me in the spring of 2014. I was twenty-four, working at the University of Missouri, and didn't have the slightest idea how much private jets cost - I just figured we'd have one some day. And you know what? I still think we could have one some day. Now don't get me wrong. I don't want to sound arrogant or ridiculous here. I think I'll be fine if I never get a private jet. I'm 6'8" so I don't exactly enjoy coach, but I'll make do. They really are a lot of money, and this book isn't about having private jets anyway. We don't care if you make a million dollars a year or $40,000. What matters is your mindset and ability to take action.

The mindset I had in that moment was a mindset fueled by abundance. This type of mindset doesn't see price tags as huge problems, but begins looking for the solutions to the obstacle. It doesn't look around and say, "All the good ideas are taken," but looks around and says, "There are so many opportunities, yet so little time."

If you're ready, let's get moving. Time to hop on the

fast track. Time to become a person who has abundance, and by abundance we don't just mean money. That might be part of it for you - or it might not. To us that means abundant friendships, abundant time, abundant energy, abundant laughter, abundant...double-stuffed Oreos (Those things are amazing).

Beyond The Grind is the track of life in which people determine the life they've always wanted to live, and then they make choices and take action to get themselves there. It doesn't matter to us where you are, it's about where you are going.

But keep this in mind that Beyond The Grind isn't really about a book. It's about a movement of fellow men and women who want more in life. We want you to be engaged in the Beyond The Grind community even after you're finished with this book. We want to you to be plugged into the wave of people like yourselves. So we're building a home for all of us. Check out getbeyondthegrind.com or more info. We're giving all the early adopters a little something extra. Don't miss it.

You ready?

Time to live **Beyond The Grind**.

CHAPTER TWO

VACATIONS ARE NICE, BUT THEY WON'T CHANGE YOUR LIFE

I'm Chris, and I've always been a dreamer. I like to think into the future and have a vision for who I want to be and what I want to do. And while forward-thinking is a great quality, there has been a downside to it for me. As I look into the future, I can come up with some pretty stellar dreams. Those dreams turn into realistic opportunities, and I feel obligated to take advantage of them - all of them. Then, when any of the 100 opportunities (or so I think) don't materialize, I get discouraged. I'll begin thinking of all the time I just wasted and all the hours I spent planning and hoping - only to return to square one. Soon after, I'll dream up more opportunities and begin pursuing them, and the trend continues. Here's one thing I've learned. The journey of life isn't a cycle; it's a progressive line forward and no time is wasted.

Where you are now is NOT where you will end up.

As simple as that statement seems, it has been extremely helpful as I look into the future. Here is the reality of life: *it changes*. When I was in college, my mentor helped me design "dream statements" for the next five years of my life. I would think of ten dream scenarios for my life, write them down in the past tense as if I'd completed them, and write actionable goals for each of them. While it's an incredible habit to form, over the last five years, I've had to readjust those goals because my life has changed dramatically. When I wrote them, they made no mention of living in India for three years, working in Atlanta, starting a software company, getting married, moving to Annapolis, or getting a dog. I couldn't possibly imagine those things happening in my life, yet they did. And while I'm so glad those changes happened, it reminds me that *where I am now is NOT where I'll end up*. The reality of life is that in five to ten, and even twenty years from now, you will be in a different place.

Regardless of how life seems right now, it's inspiring to realize that change is possible, and inevitably, change will happen. That's just the way life works.

Defining Freedom and Striving for Purpose

As Dave and I were sitting at Baltimore Tea and Coffee drinking far too many lattes and discussing this book, we kept thinking about the question, "What is true freedom?" I think that's an interesting question because the world has conditioned us to think of freedom differently than what I believe true freedom actually is.

When you think of freedom, what is your first thought? The first two words that came to my mind were retirement and the beach. When I think of freedom, I imagine someone being completely detached from the stresses of the world, being able to do anything they want, and not worrying about the outcomes. You might relate, but why was it in college (when I had this environment), I couldn't wait to get out and start working in the real world. Then the moment I stepped into the real world, I was dying to get to retirement. Since retirement was at least thirty years away, I was determined to create a profession where I could sit on the beach, read books, and have that "freedom." That was my end goal - and I was wrong. I didn't have a proper understanding of freedom.

Consider this story from Dave and see if you relate.

It depends on what kind of mood I'm in, but there's a really good chance if you ask, "Dave, what do you think of cruises?" I'll say something along the lines of, "Meh. Went on one a few years back. Great people, great food, probably won't do it again." After I graduated from college, three of my best friends and I decided to go on a cruise thanks to the generosity of one guy's mom (Thanks, Mrs. Flack). Don't get me wrong. It was a fun and cool experience, but we spent five days playing cards on the back of the ship, walking around looking for the mythical basketball court that was promised on the website and dreaming about all the things we would be doing if we were on land. We finally had "true freedom" and were basically living the retired life, yet we wanted something different.

A few years later, I hear of my friend Marcus coming back from a trip to El Salvador. It was hot, it was dirty, and he dug a big well for a week in a village. That's starting to make the cruise look pretty good, right? I came back from the cruise saying "It was nice, but I'll never do it again," and he came back from the purpose-driven trip saying, "It changed my life, and I can't wait to go back." Kind of makes you question what true freedom and purpose are, doesn't it? Marcus is heading back this March to lead a trip and this time, I'm making sure I'm going with him -even if we don't get to play much cards.

Think of all the spring break stories you hear about. In college, most of my fraternity brothers would spend the week in Panama City Beach. They'd always return with a ton of crazy stories, but I never heard this, "Wow Chris, that trip changed my life. You need to go spend a week there immediately." That never, ever happened. In fact, it was more like, "Dang Chris, that was a fun, rough week. It's good to be back in Stillwater."

Vacations are nice, but they won't change your life!

Action Step:

Stop and think through some of the vacations taken by people you know. When they returned, what did they say? What were the highlights? Does the vacation on the beach sound like a true definition of freedom in your mind, or do you have bigger plans?

This book is filled with action steps. To download the free Action Guide containing all the action items, head over to

getbeyondthegrind.com/action

Ray and I Relaxing in Dubai:

I lived in India for three years, and while it's a great place of adventure, it can be a tough place to live. Every few months I would have the thought, "Can I go back to America please? I just want good coffee, consistent electricity, and a Wendy's double-cheeseburger." And while those luxuries weren't available in India, my roommate Ray and I did find the Middle East's land of milk and honey.... Dubai! I had never planned on visiting Dubai until I learned it had everything I wanted in life - Starbucks, McDonalds, air-conditioning, and the beach.

Ray and I loaded up our backpacks, booked a flight, grabbed sunscreen, and headed to Dubai for two weeks. I was so excited about this trip. There was going to be no email, no staff reports, and no agenda. Ray and I are similar travelers and both creatures of habit, so it was easy for us to get our daily game plan.

1. Wake up at 8:55am to sprint downstairs to the Holiday Inn's complimentary breakfast that ends at 9am.

2. Eat as fast as we could and head back to bed.

3. Wake-up and pound several cups of coffee for our "big day."

4. Go to the beach for an hour (FYI: Dubai in the summer is NOT where you want to be - unbelievably hot!)

5. Head to McDonalds for our daily Big Mac.

6. Back to the hotel for a power nap.

7. Go sight-seeing for a bit, because that's what you do on vacation.

8. Drive around downtown Dubai blasting John Mayer's new CD.

9. Bed.

10. Rinse and repeat......for 14 straight days.

Looking back on that trip, the criteria of the initial "freedom" I envisioned were completely met.

Being detached from the stresses of the world ..... check

Being able to do anything I want ..... check

Not worrying about the outcomes ..... check

Life-changing experience ..... ehh, not quite

Where's the disconnect? What were we missing?

Purpose creates freedom.

Striving for Freedom Inhibits Purpose

Dave and I believe that if we strive for freedom as an end goal, we'll end up with an empty life. It might seem gratifying in the short-term, but it's never sustainable. We'll always be looking for more. We can get so consumed with creating this life of freedom that we lose focus on our natural gifts and pursuing opportunities that we are actually good at. I've always sought freedom in the sense of sitting on the beach, sipping margaritas, and having no agenda. But just like my trip to Dubai, that gets old and boring. It's empty, because there are only so many books you can read until you're left wondering, "What's next?" And I would have continued asking that question until I could shift my mindset away from striving for freedom.

Striving for Purpose Creates Freedom

When we strive for purpose we find freedom because we are using the gifts we've been given and putting them into action to add value to society. That's where our life is changed! In the world's eyes, it's a counter-intuitive thought, but purpose creates freedom because you are now able to live the life that you were made to live.

Dave didn't come back from his Bahama's cruise and and think "Wow, that trip changed my life." I didn't come back from my two-week vacation in Dubai and think, "I've got to give all my friends my itinerary and send them to Dubai ASAP." No, it's always those trips to a homeless shelter in downtown Atlanta, or a summer in Latin America digging wells, or even a week in Haiti building houses that we rave about. Why? Because vacations are necessary for rest, but not to instill vision and purpose for the future. If we strive to create a life in that "vacation-mode," we'll soon realize the future is bleak. But that can easily be changed!

Discover Your 20 Mile March

One of my favorite books is called **Good to Great**. The premise of the book is that it's not possible for everyone to be above average, but some are. The author explains the key principles of why companies go from being good to being great. Tucked away in the book is an inspiring story that has changed my life. It's called the "20 Mile March", and it's the story of explorers Roald Amundsen and Robert Falcon Scott in their efforts to lead their teams roughly 1400 miles and be the first to the South Pole in October, 1911. They had the same goal, but very different strategies.

Scott's Strategy: *Progress according to circumstances.* They were to travel <u>only</u> on the good weather days, but on those days to travel as far as they could. This made sense because the good weather days would be less taxing on their body and mind, allowing them to travel further. They could even rest on bad weather days to build up stamina and recover from the long trek.

Amundsen's Strategy: *Consistent daily progress.* They were to travel 20 miles <u>every day</u> regardless of the weather. If it was raining - 20 miles. If it was snowing - 20 miles. If it was perfect sunshine - 20 miles. Even on days when they felt energized and could do more, they stopped at 20 miles.

The Result: Amundsen's team made it exactly on time and Scott's team made it there, but... ran out of supplies and never made it home.

One team made consistent progress every day and the other group made short bursts as they felt able. The 20-mile march team was happier, more productive, and more consistent in the long term.

In regard to your dreams, which team are you on? Do you dream of a different life, take action in spurts, but find yourself stuck year after year? Or do you make a plan and create actionable goals you can meet? It's time you discover your 20 mile march.

Action Step:

Think through what you want your life to look like in 5 years. What actions do you need to start taking today to get there? Write down one action step you can take every single day for the next 30 days and commit to it.

The Commute That Changed My Life

I was 25 and wanted to live the dream. I returned from India and started work for a leadership company in Atlanta called, *Growing Leaders*. It was my first time in corporate America and I had a lot to learn. I just didn't know commuting to that job would change my life.

I wanted to maximize the 45-minute commute, so a coworker, Jake, gave me a list of podcasts. One particular morning, I randomly found a podcast explaining smart passive income and how to build a career around it. It was an interview with the founder of *The Foundation*. He explained how their company equips people to create any software company...from scratch... with no idea... and no money. Although I currently had a great job, the thought of starting a company really excited me. The problem was that I had no real professional experience, no idea how to start a company, a dwindling savings account, and no reasonable first step - until now.

This *Foundation* guy had just explained my ideal life

and now he wanted to mentor me - and it would only cost half of my entire savings account? It seemed logical and I joined the Foundation in August. It was an experience that helped shape the trajectory of my future.

After joining *The Foundation*, I dove right in and thought that, barring any major setbacks, I'd have a successful software company in about 2-3 months. I just needed the tools, the email templates, and the software developers. Once I joined *The Foundation*, they started by constantly pressing into this idea of mindset. I was naive and thought, "I have the right mindset. I can easily do this. Just give me the templates and let me go to work". I've learned that processes and reasoning are not strengths of mine. I just want someone to give me the action steps, and I'll figure it out along the way. That's exactly what happened. I skimmed over the mindset portion of the course and was soon inundated with PDF after PDF on how to start a business. If we fast forward two years, I'm still pursuing a software company, but it's not making money and might not for another six months. It could take a total of two years until this business is built, which is one year and nine months longer than I thought it would take.

The reason is simple - I didn't have the proper mindset. Dave and I were sitting at that same coffee shop in Annapolis and he made an interesting statement.

"One of the reasons I don't think my software company has really worked yet is because I don't think I'm the type of person who can handle the successes of a company, but

I'm getting closer."

Initially, Dave and I didn't expect that starting a company would completely change and shape who we were, but that's exactly what happened. We may never make millions with our companies, but we are becoming the type of people who aren't afraid to dream and follow through. I may never build a successful software company. I may never work a job where I earn residual income. And I may never get the chance to mentor others in these life principles. Regardless of those outcomes, I'm still becoming the type of person who could do it. And that's what keeps me going!

CHAPTER THREE

YOU KNOW, I DIDN'T EVEN KNOW I HAD THOSE FEELINGS

Growing up, I didn't have great self-awareness and wasn't really taught where to find my personal value. I had no idea who "Chris" really was. Society doesn't teach us that -although it sure would be helpful. We are taught to pursue everything, find what we're good at, and stick to it. The problem with that concept is that most of what you're good at is a result of your external circumstances. For example, my father is a high-school football coach. He's not just an ordinary coach either, but in the Hall of Fame and one of the best football minds around. As a result, the majority of my childhood involved sports, specifically the game of football. I was naturally educated in sports and my ability (somewhat) matched that. I was able to understand concepts that most kids my age couldn't. My upbringing gave me a distinct advantage on the field. I followed the society-driven philosophy of "Find what you're good at and stick with it." I probably took it too far because I didn't do much of anything else besides play sports. And if I wasn't playing sports, I was watching it - it was my life. Don't get me wrong, I am a firm believer in organized sports. The qualities and life lessons I've gained from sports are invaluable, but my ability to throw a spiral wasn't going to take me very far. I couldn't put all my stock in that.

What happened when I graduated from high-school and realized that a 5'8", 165- pound quarterback doesn't have a thriving future in college sports? I was lost. That's a bit of an overstatement because my parents did do a great job of setting me up for success in college. Confused is a better word. But why did I feel that way? I think it's because my personal value had been derived from a childhood of perceived value in athletic ability, but that was insufficient because it had nothing to do with my true identity and who I really am.

Psycho-Cybernetics

That's a pretty intimidating word, huh? You won't find it on a 5th-grade spelling bee list. A friend recommended that I learn the concepts of psycho-cybernetics, so I bought a book, read the title, and thought, "This is going to be a tough read." And I was correct. For the sake of simplicity, the term psycho-cybernetics means, "using your brain to steer you towards a target or goal."

In the 1960's there was a doctor from Columbia University named Maxwell Maltz who first coined the term. Psycho-Cybernetics was considered the original science of self-improvement. I don't agree with every concept Dr. Maltz proposes, but he did have several intriguing thoughts that will be beneficial to us.

Our self-image is the foundation of our entire personality.

Dr. Maltz explains, that whether we realize it or not, each of us carries within us a mental picture of ourselves - our self-image. We define our own self-image as "the sort of person I am" and it is built from our own beliefs about ourselves. These beliefs are formed by past experiences, good or bad, and the way other people have reacted to us. What's interesting is that once a belief about ourselves goes into our self-image, it becomes truth as far as we are concerned. We never question its validity, but rather proceed to live life as if it were true. We go through life "acting like" the sort of person we conceive ourselves to be.

Our self-image has complete control over our ability to achieve (or fail to achieve) any goal.

Something interesting happens after we've established our self-image and begin living life accordingly. Dr. Maltz explains that all our experiences immediately seem to verify and thereby strengthen our self-image. For example: the person who perceives themselves to be a "failure-type person" will find some way to fail, in spite of all their good intentions or willpower. Why? Because that person believes that they are a failure-type person.

Dr. Maltz states, "Whatever is difficult for you, whatever frustrations you have in your life, they are likely proving and reinforcing something ingrained in your self-image like a groove in a record." Because of this objective "proof," it very seldom occurs to us that our trouble lies in our self-image or our own evaluation of ourselves. Therefore, it becomes impossible to reach goals that you don't believe "a person like you" could ever achieve. Contrary to that, any goal is attainable by someone who believes "someone like me" could reach them.

Action Step:

Think about your own life. Is there a false self-image you are operating out of? Release that false-image! Now think about your true self and the person you desire to become. Surround yourself with people, books, and experiences that will daily mold you into the best version of you.

I'm Different From Others, and That's a Good Thing

That's the way I want to approach life. Isn't it so easy to compare our life to others? I'm learning that the better I can understand myself and how I prefer to approach life, the better off I'll be. These two tools have been valuable for me in the journey of identifying myself.

Tool #1 - The Myers-Briggs Test

I took Myers-Briggs in college, but it wasn't the first personality test I was exposed to. Around my junior year of college, it seemed like all my friends were really into the DISC profile. The only thing I remember about the DISC profile is that you fill out a questionnaire of your common traits and the test spits out an animal with the same characteristics. For example, the strong-willed, dominant person would be considered a lion and the analytical, organized person would be considered a beaver. It was fun and all, but when you're trying to make friends (or find a girlfriend), nobody wants to be the pushy lion. Therefore, every guy somehow magically becomes the calm, gentle, dependable golden retriever. The point of that story is simple. There had to be more to learn about my personality than simply claiming that I was a golden retriever. I found those answers through Myers-Briggs, and here's how it works:

You are asked to answer questions in relation to your preferences in these four specific interactions.

Interaction 1 - Favorite World

Do you prefer to focus on the outer world or on your own inner world? This would be classified as extroversion or introversion.

Interaction 2 - Information

Do you prefer to focus on the basic information you take in or do you prefer to interpret and add meaning? This would be classified as sensing or intuition.

Interaction 3 - Decisions

When making decisions, do you prefer to first look at logic and consistency or first look at the people and special circumstances? This would be classified as thinking or feeling.

Interaction 4 - Structure

In dealing with the outside world, do you prefer a structured and decided environment or do you prefer to stay open to new information and options? This would be classified as judging or perceiving.

Based on those answers, you are then placed into a specific personality grouping. It will make sense when you complete the test because let's be honest, it will describe you far better than I ever could.

Action Step:

Take the Meyers-Briggs Test in the next 14 days. A free Meyers-Briggs test is provided in the action guide:

getbeyondthegrind.com/action

How does this apply to real-life?

Example #1 - Relationships

I don't know your current relational status (without checking Facebook), but here's an example from my life, involving my beautiful wife, Chloe! My personality type is an ENFP and Chloe is an ISFP. That might be confusing to you until you take the Myers-Briggs test, but simply stated: I'm future-oriented, while Chloe lives in the present. I find clarity through processing outwardly, while Chloe would prefer to process alone, gather her thoughts, and then revisit the conversation, and so on. Bottom line, with just two out of four "letters" different, we approach the world in totally opposite ways.

One particular night early on in our dating phase, we were at church together and the pastor talked about looking into the future, chasing your dreams, and changing the world. I left that service feeling on top of the world (remember, my personality is future-oriented and that's where I find energy). My mind was filled with every opportunity I could possibly muster up in a two hour time span, and when we returned to Chloe's house I unloaded everything that was swirling around in my head. I was on a roll and probably threw out ten different dream scenarios for our life and what that could look like-- all of which were completely new ones compared to the other half dozen I shared with her the week before. Chloe, being the gentle woman she is, listened to every one of my dreams (I now know being totally overwhelmed in that moment) and then asked a question that never crossed my mind, "That's great, but what are you going to do about it tomorrow?" (silence.... silence.... silence....)

I love having a mind bent towards the future, but the downside is that I can get so consumed with the future, that I easily forget the present. That night, Chloe's response was to find a reasonable next step, but my mind was not there. Actually, I was upset because I had just poured my heart and dreams out to her and she wanted to talk about Monday morning. She thought I sounded like a whole lot of talk, but little action. That moment led us to an incredible conversation about ourselves and how we can best support each other knowing the way we are uniquely wired.

What Could Have Happened

I don't like to think about worst-case scenarios, but do I think it's important to be aware of how misunderstanding could escalate if not handled properly. If Chloe and I never had that clarifying conversation that night, I would have likely continued to dream and never taken an action step forward. Over time, Chloe might wonder if I was discontent in our present life and if I could be trusted with our future. All of which would be a reasonable assumption based on how I talk about and approach life. The reality of life is that the majority of my "present" is Chloe. If she assumed that I wasn't content with my present, she could have naturally assumed that my discontentment was a result of her. This is an extreme case, but it does happen. The majority of miscommunication has nothing to do with differing opinions, but rather an improper understanding of each other. That's clearly not a good way to operate in life, but can be avoided with simple understanding.

Three Ways I've Changed

1. I try to think before I speak, because I know Chloe appreciates my processed thoughts.

2. Chloe understands that everything I say is not completely valid, because my outward processing is just the means to finding clarity in a situation.

3. When I dream and Chloe asks me what the next step is, I now realize she is not squashing my dreams. Her intent is to actually help me get one step closer to those dreams.

Example #2 - Professionally

Chris, if you're not married by age 30, you never will be.

Those were the words spoken to me in a conference room in Atlanta. That might seem rather harsh, but that statement has helped me see the world in a different way.

The company I worked for brought in a Myers-Briggs expert who explained to me what life as an ENFP looked like.

Chris, when the world views you, they'll see someone who is amazingly good at creating ideas, extremely interested in lots of things that are happening, and can generate ideas for as long as you'll let them... And will have as much fun as possible with people doing it.

That honestly felt really good to hear! Thinking about life in that way creates a ton of excitement even now. For the record, he wasn't saying that people always viewed me in that way, but the healthiest version of myself would operate with those characteristics.

ENFP's are the most naturally gifted of all the types. But, the great danger of the ENFP is that they end up being the jack-of-all trades, master of none. The reason is because everything comes so easily to them. They'll start working at something using their natural talent and will have a fair degree of success. But because they are wired for future opportunities, they are always scanning the horizon for the next big thing. And the moment they come up against any type of resistance that requires commitment, they will talk themselves into the next exciting thing. And this cycle will cease only when an ENFP is disciplined enough to stay committed in the long-term.

His words caught my attention because I had never thought of the implications of being a "visionary" before.

Do you have anything or anyone to practice commitment on? If you don't, you need to start now. Because if you aren't married by the age of 30, you never will be.

That definitely wasn't something I expected to hear on a Thursday afternoon. I'm glad I was committed to Chloe so I could simply answer yes and continue on with my afternoon. Deep down though, I knew there was more to it than just being married by the age of 30. It was another reminder for me that the "grass is greener" cycle would continue for the entirety of my life unless I made a decision to commit.

That conversation has become a foundation to guiding my future, especially professionally. I'm currently in the early stages of starting a software company. In the beginning, the process was new, the work was exciting and I was about to conquer the world. Then it got difficult, and more difficult, and it's still really difficult. My natural tendency, in the midst of these challenges, has been to pack it up and start something new. But I won't. Why? Because I can't shake the conversation I had in that conference room. I'm won't give up because the carrot of "what's next" will always be dangling in front of me. And I'm just now becoming the type of person who can ignore that false hope and stay committed.

Tool #2 - The Enneagram Test

The first task I was given after joining the *Foundation* was simple: Take the Enneagram test. Being very familiar with the Myers-Briggs, I was initially skeptical about jumping right into another personality test. But what I found through the Enneagram test was depth. It didn't just explain common characteristics, but focused on the the root issues. It explained the why.

Myers Briggs (ENFP): Charismatic, great people skills, and resists conflict

Enneagram (#9 Peacemaker): Their basic desire is to have inner stability and "peace of mind."

Same person, but do you see the difference? ENFP's are good with people and are often pleasers who resist conflict. The Enneagram takes it a step further and explains why I'm good with people and why I resist conflict. The reason is because I desire peace. Things made sense after I realized this truth about myself. My basic desire was harmony with others, which gave me a natural ability to connect with others. My desire for inner peace was the root of why I fled confrontation and resisted conflict at all costs. The Enneagram allowed me to dig deeper and understand the motivations of why I was wired a certain way. This is where real life change happened with me.

Action Step:

Take the Enneagram Test within 14 days after the Myers Briggs Test. Learn more about yourself. You won't regret it!

A free Enneagram test is provided in the action guide:

getbeyondthegrind.com/action

I Didn't Even Know I Had Those Feelings

It was March 30th, 2013. I remember the date because I was on my way to meet Chloe's family in Charlotte. We had a long drive, but much to talk about. That car ride was important for our relationship, and the Enneagram had a lot to do with it.

We were in month two of dating and learning a lot about each other. I had taken the Enneagram test and thought, "Let's both take the test, print the results, and discuss it on our road trip." This was one of my better decisions because it sparked conversations that we hadn't been able to have before. The Enneagram has helped me in two ways. First, I understand myself better. Second, I know how to communicate about myself better. I was able to verbalize things about myself on that car ride that I never knew existed. Chloe probed for a deeper explanation of my desires and fears. And as we talked, I became aware that I didn't even know I had those feelings. That's the power of the Enneagram.

Why is My Personality a Triangle?

The Enneagram is made up of nine separate personality types. Each personality type is linked to two other personalities, forming a triangle. This is important because the triangle component reveals the specific characteristics of our personalities in a healthy or unhealthy state.

My personality is number nine — peacemaker. At any given moment, I'm either moving into a Direction of Disintegration (stress) or a Direction of Integration (growth). I'm either moving towards a more or less healthy version of myself. And that's where the two connected personalities come into play. For a nine, when I'm in an unhealthy state, I will suddenly become anxious and worried, which is common with sixes. But when I'm in a healthy state, I will become energetic and self-developing, which is common with threes. This is important because these behavioral triggers allow us to see whether we're operating in our true self or not. My true personality is driven by motivation and self-development. If patterns in my life head in the opposite direction, then it would be an immediate red flag. The understanding of our behavioral patterns and triggers help us address deeper issues faster and return to a healthier state of being.

The greatest skill for any person to possess is the ability to understand themselves.

Action Step:

Identify the personalities associated with your triangle component. Then write out the specific characteristics you would exhibit if you were moving into a Direction of Integration (healthy/growth) or a Direction of Disintegration (unhealthy/stress).

Finding Your Why?

Two qualities that most children acquire naturally are a constant curiosity about the world and a limitless approach to life. It's natural for them because they don't know anything about the world and curiosity helps make sense of it all. They also don't understand limits, which means that everything in life is fair game until they are told no. I wish I still had that perspective. What happens as we get older that makes us feel as if our dreams are no longer attainable? What causes our curiosity to fade and keeps us from chasing our dreams? I believe that somewhere on our journey of life we've actually forgotten our dreams. Worse yet, most of us have actually forgotten how to dream. We need to learn how to dream again.

One of my favorite quotes is from civil rights leader Howard Thurman. "Don't ask what the world needs. Ask what makes you come alive, and go do it. Because what the world needs is people who have come alive."

What is it that makes you come alive? If you're not quite sure, it's time you find your "Why Statement."

Step 1: The Foundation for Your "Why Statement"

In order for us to understand what makes us come alive, we first need to build a foundation. Here's a few questions that will prompt your thinking, and help you start dreaming again:

Questions to Ask

- What excites you?
- What types of activities do you find most enjoyable?
- What people or what kind of people energize you?
- When was the last time you had a really good day?
- What did that day look like?
- If you had no limitations, what would you do?
- If you had unlimited time, what would you do?
- If you had unlimited money, what would you buy?

Action Step:

Answer those questions, but add a column beside each response and ask, why? (why are those activities enjoyable, why do those people energize me, why would I spend my time doing this or that?) Our hope is that you won't simply remember what excites you, but why it does.

Step 2: Constructing your "Why Statement"

What do you want to do?

This answer should be a whole lot easier now that you've identified the types of things that excite you, or better yet.. make you come alive! Simply look back at your answers from step 1 and identify why you exist. This will take time, but once you've established what you want to do, write it down.

How do you want to do it?

This is the action step that will keep you moving towards that desired life outcome. I recommend making it less specific because it's not your guide for a particular situation , but for your entire life purpose.

The framework for your "why statement."

I want to _____ by _____ .

You'll simply input your answers from above and you've got a *why* statement! Start repeating your statement to gauge how you feel about it. If the statement doesn't give you sense of excitement, start over. You'll likely be tweaking your *why* statement for a while. Eventually, all the pieces will come together and you'll be amazed at how emotionally energized you feel. There is something significant about finding your purpose and taking the next step to living within it.

My Personal "Why Statement" and How I Got There

I really enjoy spending time with college students. I've spent the majority of my professional career leading and mentoring them. I think it's because a lot of them are ambitious, full of energy, and are interested in changing the world. Those are the type of people that make me feel alive. I've also learned that a significant conversation over a cup of coffee really energizes me. Some of my more enjoyable moments in life are spent at a coffee shop with someone talking about life. What energizes me during those conversations is finding ways to help that other person reach their highest poten- tial. I find great joy in being a source of inspiration for others. And that's where it gets fun for me because inspiring someone can occur in many ways. It can be through fun activities, quick notes, meaningful conversations, and the list goes on. I'm continually searching for useful avenues to communicate truth and inspiration. And that's the reason my personal why statement is:

I want to inspire others by finding useful avenues to communicate truth.

The next step is to continually adjust the trajectory of our lives to find out what makes us tick. It's important that we're certain our end goal is indeed ours and not what others or the world convinces us of. The end goal is our personal *Why*, and we have to be diligent to pursue it.

CHAPTER FOUR

WHEN IN DOUBT, FLY TO SOUTH AFRICA

There is a reason that where you are and where want to be are not the same. It's just not enough to have a clear destination. We've always had that destination. That's easy. What's hard is becoming the type of person who can get to that destination.

Life Will Give Whatever You Ask of It

Legendary speaker Tony Robbins had just finished a seminar one evening and decided to take a walk around Boston. Around midnight, he ran into a homeless man who was begging for money. The homeless man said something along the lines of, "I need a quarter. Can you be so kind to spare me that change?" Tony mulled over the decision because he didn't want to condone that type of behavior, but wanted to teach the beggar a lesson. Tony responded to the homeless man, "Are you sure that is all you want, a quarter?" The homeless man responded, "Oh yes, one quarter will change my life." Tony Robbins then reached into his left pocket, pulled out a wad of hundred dollar bills to make room and then proceeded to pull out a quarter. As the homeless man stared intently at the wad of hundreds, Tony put the hundreds back into his pocket, held out the quarter and told the beggar, "Life will give whatever you ask of it." He gave the beggar the quarter and walked away.

I secretly hope that Tony went back and gave that homeless man a few hundred dollar bills, but I'll never know. Tony's response, nonetheless, has been a key in my journey of life — *life will give whatever you ask of it*. It all starts with your mindset and how you are going to ask.

Mindset of Abundance

I first learned the importance of mindset when I joined the *Foundation*. I wanted the practical tools to start a business, but they pushed me to think bigger.

"You can do so much more than you think your capable of doing. And the mind is your power for opportunity or it could be your demise if you let it."

The *Foundation* not only challenged my thinking, but pushed me to develop an abundant mindset. Initially, I was confused because I understood abundance to be something of excess. So, if I had an abundant mindset, did I have extra mind available that could make me smarter? Eventually, I learned that it had nothing to do with the growth of your IQ, but rather the development of how you perceived the world. A lot of people look at the world and immediately see its limitations, while others look at the world and immediately see its opportunities. That's the difference. A person with a strong abundant mindset sees the promise and hope of the world, while others do not.

One of the reasons we are just introducing this concept is because we needed a proper outlook on life in order to fully develop this mindset - and not just any outlook, but one that is created by us, formed from our identity, and approaches life with a sense of excitement. How do we evaluate to see whether our mindset needs some work? It might seem simple, but if you don't feel alive, then your mindset needs to shift.

I Like The Way That Guy Thinks

Dave and I recently listened to a podcast by an entrepreneur named Ryan Fletcher. He's a popular real-estate marketer and has an interesting perspective that will be helpful as we craft our mindset of abundance. Early in his career, Ryan became fascinated with world leaders and how certain people are able to attract large followings, while others are not. As he studied, he found that the most successful leaders may not have had the best ideas, but they told the best stories. He contends that stories elicit emotion, and that's what gets to the heart of a person causing them to act. To prove his point further, Fletcher analyzed an interview with PayPal co-founder Peter Thiel. Fletcher made a fascinating discovery as he listened to Thiel answer questions throughout the interview. Peter Thiel wasn't just answering questions, but he was presenting an argument. Thiel's responses were clear and articulate. By the end of the interview, the audience was left thinking, "Huh, good point. I like the way this guy thinks." Agreeing with the way someone thinks is much more powerful than simply liking them. Fletcher credits that shift in mindset to how these successful world leaders were able to create such a large following. They were able to look at the world differently, show how others could get involved, and then communicate in a way that people were hooked because they liked the way that leader thought. And one of the most powerful ways to create a following is to get others to think the way you do.

We all look at the world differently. Some of us create our own worldview and some of us adopt the worldview of others, or it could be a combination of both. Perhaps your worldview has been shaped by your childhood, your friends, or even the books you read. Regardless, it's important to note that our worldview is personal and changing. What do the best leaders do that others don't? They have developed the ability to identify and articulate their worldview.

We are all leaders! It's easy to elevate leadership to someone on TV or on a stage, but a leader is simply anyone who affects someone else - and that includes every single one of us. Whether we are an employee, parent, teacher, coach, or friend, it's crucial for us to lead well. We all want to leave a positive impact on those around us. The better we can identify and articulate our worldview, the better the leader we can be. Why? It sets the framework for how our mind works.

Crafting a Mindset of Abundance

The early stages of crafting an abundant mindset were very difficult for me. I assumed that if I just viewed the world as a massive playground, I would be able to see opportunities that I couldn't before. As I looked at the world this way, a lingering tension accompanied those thoughts. I didn't know how I personally viewed the world. I was the person in the "worldview adopted by others" category. I had a worldview, but it wasn't fully mine. It belonged to others. I needed to develop my personal core beliefs so that I could have my own framework to view the world. Only then would I be able to start the process of crafting a mindset of abundance.

Undeniable Truths

In that same podcast, Ryan Fletcher explained an exercise to help develop a worldview. He calls them "Undeniable Truths." Ryan created a document stating his personal opinions about the world. They weren't necessarily concise, but more of "Here's a thought I had."

As he began to document these thoughts, you can imagine how quickly he filled up a page. What happens when you're looking at pages of your own opinions? You might realize you have far too many opinions, or you might start to analyze which opinions are actually true. He then took his list of opinions and began to test them. He did that by either personally disproving the thought or having someone else disprove it. The result of this was that every time he couldn't discredit a thought and every time he would present his opinion to someone else and they couldn't refute it, he gained more and more conviction to say, "This is my worldview." He did this continually until he was able to create a solid list of 35 undeniable truths.

Action Step:

Write out 3-5 of your personal opinions about the world. Next, attempt to refute these opinions either by your own logic or by someone else. Continue this exercise with several people. How many of your initial opinions will become your undeniable truths?

A Short List of Undeniable Truths
by Dave and Chris

- The world is full of endless opportunities…we just have to find them.

- Life is best enjoyed when surrounded by meaningful relationships.

- Life is most fulfilling when our work aligns both with our gifts and our passions.

- We are our own worst enemies, and must be diligent not to self-sabotage our dreams.

- Limiting beliefs are at the root of most of our shortcomings. We doubt we can really achieve success.

Building the Framework for an Abundant Mindset

Now that you've written out your undeniable truths, we use those statements to build a framework for our new mindset. This is critical because our mindset is directly correlated with our core beliefs about the world. As we continually test and gain more conviction for our core beliefs, we'll have a much more confident approach to the world.

Take each of your undeniable truths and let that be the structure for your new mindset. I gave you an example of what Dave and I came up with over a cup of coffee, but my personal core beliefs took a bit more time. I'll give you several of my undeniable truths because I think it will be more valuable for you to see how my mindset has developed over the years.

Chris' Undeniable Truths (sample)

- I can do anything, but I can't do everything

- The world is full of opportunities that are waiting to be taken

- Everyone is accessible, but I have to go find them

- I am motivated for a single cause: the ability to effect

The Development of My Mindset

It's important to note that these truths are in constant development. I mentioned earlier about using our own or someone else's logic to test our opinions, but there is one more key ingredient - life experiences. The beauty of it is that our mindset is in constant development and so are our lives. As we develop our worldview, we can insert any past or present life experience to validate that opinion. Using life experiences give us the ability to quickly validate our worldviews.

I Can Do Anything, But I Can't Do Everything

One of the luxuries of working at a leadership company is that you're constantly reminded of life principles. My boss Tim Elmore, engrained one simple truth into us whenever he referred to the power of focus:

You can do anything, but you can't do everything.

If our minds are consumed with everything, we'll end up accomplishing nothing.

Nearing the end of my third year in India, I started to transition my life and career back to the States. I was unsure of my next step, so I mapped out certain careers that I wanted to pursue. I had no problem creating a list of opportunities, but found it extremely challenging to narrow the focus. It seemed like everything that I had written down was worth pursuing, and I needed to find a way to creatively go after them all. That was my intent, but I eventually had to come to terms with the fact that it was impossible for me to pursue ten things at once. I reduced the list and decided to create a strategic plan. The strategic plan wasn't just my dreams, but also included actionable steps for each opportunity.

- Partner with Kunal to develop exercise programs to use in Indian schools

- Develop the curriculum for an Indian sports leadership company

- Start a global staffing company to employ Americans internationally

- Become an administrator at a college football program

- Train international cricket teams through mental conditioning

I'll spare you the action steps, but I felt confident in that list because every dream had real potential. The issue was that as much as I wanted to, there was no way I could have achieved those goals simultaneously. Instead of simply choosing one of them, I wanted to pursue all of them. And nothing happened. I'm constantly reminded that if I chase after everything, I'll never end up accomplishing anything. The power of commitment and focus are key in life and to remember that I can do anything, but I can't do everything.

The World Is Full Of Opportunities That Are Waiting to Be Taken

In the *Foundation*, I was taught to always put on my green glasses. It sounded strange, but it reminded me to do two things. First, I needed look at the world differently than I currently was (hence the glasses). And secondly, look at the world without limits (hence the green and not red). They repeated that phrase to remind me that it's our natural tendency to look at the world with a limited scope, rather than seeing abundance everywhere. To this day, that visual helps me remember that the world is indeed full of opportunities. Being the type of person who can find them is the challenging part. And that's where I'm growing. This is how it's played out for me:

I need someone to give me an opportunity

I need to find any opportunity

I need to find the right opportunity

I need to look for opportunity in all circumstances.

Growing up, I was extremely fortunate and had parents that supported and provided for my every need. In fact, most things actually came to me. I got my first job when I was sixteen years old and had three more before I left for college. I never set up a job interview for any one of them; I just happened to be helpful at the right time and was hired on the spot. So during my adolescence, I was never in a situation where I needed to make things happen for myself. Therefore, initiating and finding opportunities were somewhat foreign to me. If anything, I felt that if I just kept being helpful, someone would give me a chance.

I mentioned this earlier, but my transition back to the States was difficult. I was excited and searching for a career, but needed someone to give me an opportunity - and nobody did. This was new territory and I didn't know what to do. I attempted to work the connections I had, however, it just didn't happen. As time progressed and pressure increased, I was desperate to find something and went from "I need someone to give me an opportunity" to "I need to find any opportunity." As I started looking for any opportunity, most of them didn't make a lot of sense. I even considered going back to India without friends and family, which isn't ideal. I took a deep breath and knew that I had to make decisions from the standpoint of "I need to find the right opportunity." And that's where I feel like I'm most often in.

To work in Atlanta and start a software company felt like the right opportunity. And while it was definitely the "right opportunity", I often wonder where I'd be if I were wearing my green glasses at that time. The world is a different place for me now than it was at that time. I have a better grasp on "looking for opportunity in all circumstances" because the world is full of them. Yet, those with an abundant mindset always approach life in that manner. I'm hopefully getting closer to seeing those opportunities and taking them, rather than waiting to see what happens. It seems like good always happens when we initiate and go after things, and it's those experiences that help remind me that the world is full of opportunities that are waiting for me to take.

Everyone is Accessible, but I Have To Go Find Them

When I was living in India, I had a dream to connect with the most influential people in the country. It seemed difficult, but I was young, ambitious, and had "being an American" working to my advantage. As it turned out, it was a lot more difficult than I envisioned. I didn't give up, but had to get more strategic. I first thought about who the most influential people in the country were. That was easy - the Indian cricket team. Cricket is by far the most popular sport in India and the players are the face of the country. The Indian cricket team is the equivalent of the Olympic basketball team .... multiplied by 100. I didn't take long to realize my chance to meet those players were slim to none and decided to pursue the next best option - the coach.

I started researching and found that India typically hires coaches from other countries to lead their national teams. India's cricket coach, Paddy, was born in South Africa. At the time, he was coaching the South African national team, and also founded a mental performance company.

In all of my research, I gathered one very important item: an e-mail address. I spent the day crafting the perfect e-mail about myself, my aspirations, how Paddy fits into those, etc. And the response was absolutely nothing. I continued to send follow-up emails, but got the same silent response time after time. I was on the brink of calling it quits when I had one last thought, "What if I fly to Cape Town and see if I can find him?" As I sat in my apartment in India, I sent him one last e-mail along the lines of "I'm going to be in Cape Town next week. Would you like to grab a quick lunch?" The next morning came, and to my complete surprise, he had responded and said sure. I immediately got on Kayak.com, booked a flight to Cape Town, and was there within a few days.

On the trip, I spent several hours with Paddy learning about his life, cricket, and those Indian players. And while the process of getting that two-hour lunch seems a little crazy, it's had a huge impact on me. It led to a friendship with Paddy and gave me a larger perspective to view the world. I never got connected to the Indian cricket team, but I learned more than that. That experience further validated for me that everyone is accessible, but I have to go find them. When in doubt, fly to South Africa!

I Am Motivated for a Single Cause: the Ability to Affect

Now you know that my personal *Why* statement is to inspire others. Looking back, I realize the thought of inspiring or positively affecting others has been the motivation for most of my life decisions. It's been there even before I put it into a fancy statement. The reason I moved to India was because of a desire to help change lives for the better. I worked in Atlanta to learn how to best lead the next generation. I started a company to give me a platform to serve others. I'm writing this book to help others think differently. My desire to positively affect others has always been there, but I'm learning how to do it best.

My time in Atlanta made for an incredible experience for a couple of reasons. The most important reason being that I got to meet my beautiful wife. The second most important reason is that I was mentored on how to lead and invest in the next generation effectively. I was drawn to this company in Atlanta because I wanted to know how to lead better. I felt that my ability to affect others was directly correlated with my ability to lead. The better I lead, the larger impact I make. That was the motivation. During that time, I received some of the best advice on leadership I've ever heard. He's humble and would never say this, but my former boss, Tim Elmore, is the world's primary thought leader on next generation leadership. I've never met anyone who understands leadership like he does.

I'll never forget one conversation. I had just decided to leave his company and start my software business. Because it was nearing the end of my time there, I was trying to learn as much as possible, as fast as possible. Tim and I were talking about life and before we ended, I had one last question, and I'm sure glad I asked it. "If you could instill specific qualities into the next generation, what would you give them?" I was expecting a pause or that he would take a moment to think, but he didn't. He quickly responded by saying, "That's easy. I would give students the ability to serve people and to solve problems. If we had a world filled with those types of young people, we'd be looking at an extremely bright future."

Wow! If my time working for him boiled down to that one question, it was well worth it. That was all I needed to know. If I wanted to influence the next generation, I had to teach them those two qualities. But before I could teach them, I needed to make sure my life was a representation of that. This is now my life motivation. I want to be a man that serves people and solves problems. It gives me the greatest opportunity to positively affect someone else.

When I joined *The Foundation* and started the sales module training, I was pumped. I was about to learn proven cold call sales tactics and how to write the perfect email. This was how I would make the big bucks! Instead, I was taught something else - sales is asking to serve people. I didn't expect to start off with that, but isn't that a great way to think of sales? Instead of knocking on doors and asking people to buy a product, you approach them with the mindset of serving them. Approaching sales as an opportunity to serve provides the best chance to positively affect someone else. That made a lot of sense to me, and that's how I began my software company.

My software business currently serves physical therapists. When I chose this market, I knew nothing other than there were 30,000 therapists in the US. That's a lot of people to serve. So what did I do? I didn't have a product and had no idea what a physical therapist actually did, so I couldn't sell them anything. Instead, I started calling and emailing thousands of therapists across the country asking them one question.

"What are the biggest challenges you face in your day?"

Do you see how this approach is different than most salesman? And what was the result? The answers came flooding in. When I asked about their daily challenges and demonstrated genuine interest in their lives, I was able to take the sales tactic of building rapport to a whole new level. I wasn't asking them to buy anything, so they knew there wasn't a sneaky catch. I was simply trying to figure out a way to make their lives better. If I could do that, great. Even if I couldn't, I had just made new friends and learned about their lives.

Today, I'm connected to more physical therapists than I could have ever imagined, and we are working towards that ideal world of generating income to make their lives easier. Whether or not I get there, I hope that my sales approach of serving them will at least leave a good impression. I was at a conference where a Fortune 500 CEO made this statement, "Your role as a business owner is not to make money, but to positively affect people and positively affect the world. If you do that, the money will come." That's how I want to approach business.

Those two stories (and more like them) have been hugely impactful in my life. It's helped me to realize the underlying motivation for why I want to inspire others. Every time I have these types of experiences, I remember this truth further validating that I am motivated for a single cause: *the ability to affect.*

CHAPTER FIVE

NO ONE TALKS TO YOU MORE THAN YOU TALK TO YOU

Keeping the Mindset of Abundance

Have you ever wondered why it's so hard to keep a new habit or skill? Maybe it's because we get busy, or we get lazy, or we just forget to hone it. As we acquire new skills, it's important to remember that once we have it, it's essential to keep practicing. The development of our abundant mindset is absolutely no different. The moment we think we have this whole abundance thing figured out, there's a good chance we'll lose it. Since it's not our natural way of thought, we have to fight to keep it. I think there are three specific actions we can take that will give us the best chance to do just that.

1. Removing the obstacles in our lives

2. Reversing the limiting beliefs about ourselves

3. Consistent self-talk

Removing The Obstacles in Our Lives

A couple of years ago, I read a book called *Necessary Endings* written by a psychologist named Henry Cloud. In the book, he explains that our tendency is to put a lot of thought and energy into the things we need or want to be doing. He challenges that tendency and poses these two questions:

- Have you considered what you should stop doing?

- Are there endings that you need to make in order to achieve what you want in life?

Dr. Cloud would contend that while endings are a necessary part of life, we often avoid them or mess them up. He then compares the process of necessary endings to a gardener pruning a bush. I don't know anything about flowers besides the fact that Chloe's favorites are hydrangeas. (Pro Tip: know your girl's favorite flower!) What I have learned is that one rose bush can produce a variety of flowers, and it's through the process of pruning that a gardener can grow the best flowers. There are three reasons a gardener prunes a rose bush.

1. The bush produces more buds than it can sustain, which means the good buds need to be pruned to make room for the best.

2. A bud isn't growing, even after providing more sunlight, vitamins, fertilizer, or any other treatment.

3. A bud is dead and is simply taking up space.

That makes sense, but what does this have to do with our mindset? I think Step 1 for us is simply being aware of the pruning that will need to happen in order for us to stay committed to this new mindset. Also, pruning comes by continually asking these three questions in regards to our new worldview.

1. Am I involved in good things that keep me from being fully involved in the best things?

2. What in my life is not changing even after my best efforts?

3. Are there areas of my life that take time and energy, but serve no purpose?

Action Step:

Revisit the three parts of the pruning process and write down the answers to those questions. It will help you identify certain areas of your life that could use some pruning. You might be surprised at the things that seem good, but are actually keeping you from reaching your full potential. At least I was!

Reversing the Limiting Beliefs About Ourself

I believe that knowing your limiting beliefs and learning the power of reversing them could be the key to reaching your ultimate potential. Psychologists say that there are two types of beliefs: *empowering* and *limiting*.

While it is true that some beliefs empower us and others limit us, there has got to be a reason. I know that those feelings are a response to something deeper. I wonder if the feeling of empowerment or limitation could be changed if we dug deeper? What if we were able to get to the core of those beliefs? If we knew the actual reasons for our belief, could we shift our mind in a way that results in feeling empowered, rather than limited? There is a way to do this; its called *reversing your limiting beliefs*. Below we'll give you a framework to work through these limiting beliefs.

You start by asking these two questions to identify a limiting belief.

1. What is a goal I have?

Example: *I want to exercise regularly*

2. Why haven't I reached it yet?

I'm too busy with work. I don't have enough time. I don't have the energy.

You've just found a limiting belief: **I don't have enough time to exercise regularly.**

Next, work through the following questions.

1. Is this belief true?

Yes, I don't have enough time to exercise regularly.

2. Is this belief always true? Is it possible there is at least one person on the planet that could prove this wrong?

Of course it's not always true. There are millions of working individuals who find enough time to exercise on a regular basis.

3. How does this belief make me feel?

When I think about this belief, I feel frustrated and helpless. It's frustrating because I want to get in shape, but I'm not doing anything about it. The gyms are filled up, but I'm not there. Why am I not able to do what others do? I'm frustrated because time actually is limited and I can't fit exercise into an already busy schedule. That makes me feel helpless because there is nothing I can do with my work schedule. My free time, which is typically spent exercising, is in the hands of my boss.

4. What would the opposite of this belief be?

I have more than enough time to exercise if I'm strategic with my day. Actually, limited time forces me to be more creative and structured with my weekly plans. If I plan well, it will give me time to exercise and likely even more time in the evenings to spend with friends.

You've just found your empowering belief: **I have more than enough time to exercise if I'm strategic with my day.**

1. How does this empowering belief make me feel?

I feel joyful because the day is long and I can spend it in meaningful ways. This excites me and I'm ready to start planning my day.

2. What choice will I make today to ensure I keep this belief ?

I will go on a 15 minute jog on my lunch break.

Isn't that an interesting way to approach goals? It's the same goal with a completely different process. The limiting belief creates frustration and helplessness and the new empowering belief creates joy and excitement. When we live through empowering beliefs, we are more likely to reach the end goal. This process is crucial to keep an abundant mindset. There is no denying that doubts will come. And there is a good chance we'll have a long list of excuses lined up waiting to join forces with them. However, if we can identify and reverse the limiting beliefs about ourselves, we'll improve our chances to stand firm and stay committed to our goals.

Going Deeper

In order to get to the heart of real life change, we have to dig down and work on our deep limiting beliefs. I once heard a story about a woman who wanted to lose weight. She had tried everything, but just couldn't get herself to eat healthy and exercise. It was totally ruining her life, so she went to a counselor for some help. The counselor identified the problem when the woman kept explaining all the things she had tried and failed. The counselor asked a few probing questions and helped her to realize what she truly thought about herself. She believed she was an overweight and unhealthy person. That was her limiting belief. It didn't matter if she made a schedule for jogging - she couldn't keep it. Why? Because unhealthy and overweight people typically don't keep strict jogging schedules. As long as that's who she was, and that's what she believed was true, she couldn't change. She had to change what she believed about herself.

The counselor helped her ingrain one simple thought into her brain. That one simple thought would reverse her woes - "I am an athlete." At first, she didn't believe the thought at all. She kept trying it on, but it just never felt comfortable. It was so different from what she had believed for years. But she persevered. The more she tried it on, the more it began to fit - and she began to jog. The more she jogged, the more that thought became a belief and felt true. She began to eat healthy. Not because she had to or she had some cleverly designed system to trick her.

She began eating healthy, because that's what athletes do! Before long she was jogging regularly, eating primarily healthy foods, and signed up for a marathon. She ended up losing all the excess weight and now plans her vacation time at work around various marathons across the county. Quite literally, she is an athlete.

Personally, I often find myself not following through with things. It's not so much my actions that limit me, but often times I don't believe I'm the type of person who can follow through. I can get all the way to the end of a project and just crush it, but that last 10% is unbelievably tough. Because when I get there, a core belief about myself is that I'm not a person who can finish this - and so I often bail, and leave things unfinished.

Without getting too scientific here, beliefs like this are stored in the deeper part of our brain that doesn't respond well to logic or words. Words can get the process moving, like in the case of the female athlete story, but our brain will snap back quickly unless we encounter new experiences. New experiences program and reprogram the part of our brain that hold these core beliefs. In my case, I can make progress by telling myself, "I'm a person who follows through," but the real change comes when I recognize that I've completed something. Then I can look back and say, "Of course, I'm a follow-through type person - look at what I just followed through on!"

This is a cycle that is continually repeated until the brain literally and physically reprograms itself to believe the new belief. This is called neuro-plasticity. Take some time and try it.

What is holding back your life in significant ways?

Here are a few thoughts we've wrestled through. See if you can relate.

1. *If people really knew me, they wouldn't like me.*

(This thought will hold you back from becoming close with people)

2. *I am stupid and can't do anything right.*

(This one might come from parental/authority figures in your life)

3. *I am not lovable.*

(This one really hurts and will keep you isolated)

4. *I'm not a person people want to follow.*

(This may hold you back from stepping into leadership positions for which you are qualified)

5. *I'm not someone people can depend on.*

(Will cause you to let people down a lot - despite your

best intentions)

It may take you lots of time and emotional energy to really find the beliefs that drive your negative behavior, but I can guarantee that when you do, and you take steps to understand and reverse those - you'll be set free in ways you never thought possible. You'll begin to see yourself in a whole new light, and the reality you've always dreamt of will become the reality that you live. You will be a happy, healthy, lovable, following-through, dependable, likable person.

Consistent Self-Talk

Here's what happens to me almost every night. It gets to be about 11pm and since that's when most responsible humans go to bed, I figure it's time to start winding down.

Unfortunately, the winding down process is a bit complicated for me - unless Tylenol PM is involved. I will lay in bed for hours looking at the ceiling until I finally fall asleep. During those hours of "ceiling watching," my mind is racing. It's really hard for me to turn my mind off, especially late at night when there are no distractions. It seems like all my thoughts from the day pile up, and I'm forced to analyze them at the most inopportune time (i.e. bedtime). As I think about those late nights, I realize that my mind is actually always racing. It's just late at night where it becomes more evident. This might sound strange, but do you realize that we talk to ourselves constantly? A church leader named Matt Chandler describes the idea of self-talk like this:

You are constantly talking to you. **No one talks to you more than you talk to you.** In fact, every moment of the day, whether you're aware of it or not, you're talking to you. So you are constantly whispering things to yourself, speaking to yourself, and driving yourself in certain directions by what you say to yourself. You talk to yourself when you're listening to music, when you're watching movies, and even during conversations with others. It's always there. And probably when you're most dialed into your inner voice is when you finally put your head on the pillow at night.

Isn't it interesting that one of the greater influences in our approach to life is our inner voice. How we talk to ourselves has a huge effect on our decision-making and where we end up. Here are three mindset-shifting truths about self-talk.

1. *We think about ourselves much more than others think about us.*

(If that's true, then our opinion of ourself is what matters, not what others think of us)

2. *If we are already feeding our mind thoughts constantly, they might as well be valuable.*

(Our words matter. We can choose to feed our mind valuable thoughts or not)

3. *We can achieve (or not achieve) certain things in life based on how we talk to ourselves.*

(If self-talk guides our decision-making, then we must make sure it's pointing us in the right direction.)

I made this the final action on the list because it's really the culmination of everything we've discussed. I mentioned this earlier, but it's just not enough to start developing a new mindset of abundance. We have the practical tools to help us get there, but that's the easy part. What's hard is becoming the type of person who can *keep* that mindset. Only through consistent practice and self-talk can we hold onto and continue developing this mindset.

You will likely put this book down, turn on the TV, and get sucked back into the craziness of life. However, if we consistently remember who we are, why we exist, and how to approach the world, what will we be filling our mind with? We'll feed our brain valuable insight that gives us the best chance to live the way we were designed. I don't know about you, but I want to talk to myself about those types of things. It would make those sleepless nights a bit more meaningful.

Action Step:

We can choose to feed our mind with valuable thoughts or not. What's one way you'll feed your mind this week (books, conversations, etc) that will have a positive impact on the future of your life?

CHAPTER SIX

INITIATIVE IT ONLY HURTS AT FIRST

Successful people all have one thing in common that they do really well. They take initiative, and they take loads of it. I've never really liked when people make absolute statements like "Initiative is the *most* important quality of a leader" so I won't say it here, but initiative is right up towards the top.

Think of the most successful people that you personally know. Think about how they live life. Do they wait for opportunities to come to them or do they go out and take what they want? I guarantee that they take what they want. I guarantee they take action on ideas. I guarantee they take initiative towards life day after day after day. And you know what? It works, regardless of the situation.

The Enemy of Initiative

I'll be the first to say that initiative is exhausting. Chris and I both held jobs after college where we were the ones initiating contact with people 95% of the time. Hardly anyone initiated back. If we sat at home, no one was going to call us. No one was going to poke their head in and say "Hey." Nothing was going to get done without us stepping up and making it happen.

Every morning I had to make a conscious decision that only I would ever know about. I had to decide, "Am I going to take initiative today, or am I going to be passive and watch the world go by?" I hate to say it, but I definitely chose passivity more often than I'd like, and I'm still paying for it today. Passivity is never free. It's easy, but it isn't free. It has an incredibly high price tag that can be measured in opportunity cost. The New Oxford American Dictionary defines opportunity cost as "the loss of potential gain from other alternatives when one alternative is chosen."

Whoa. Let's consider that again. "The loss of potential gain from other alternatives when one alternative is chosen."

This means that all of those times when I just didn't make the call and hoped someone would call me, the times I waited around because I didn't have the "perfect" idea - those had a cost. I took a loss, when potential gain was available. Thinking back to that really hits me hard. Laziness and passivity don't seem like a big deal in the moment, but they are incredibly costly. Passivity is always so much more attractive than initiative in the moment.

Think about your life now. What are the biggest

opportunities you've missed out on lately? If you'd taken initiative would you have a different job than you have now? Would you be going to a better school than you are now? Would you have a close friend that you've now lost touch with? Would you have better health than you do? Would you have a small business started by now?

I don't list all of those things to beat you up. If you are beating yourself up right now and feeling shame - stop. That won't help. That's part of the problem. I list those things to inspire you. Mistakes aren't a bad thing. Mistakes not learned from are the problem.

Failure: The Key to Success

Let me just say something before we move any further into the book. If you are too afraid to take initiative because of the fear that you might fail, then the rest of this book isn't for you. The rest won't help. You need to stop and look within and really work on those limiting beliefs you have that make you too afraid to move forward. More books aren't going to help you; you've got to dig deep and fix some underlying thoughts about yourself. But for those of you who think you could eek out even just a little bit of action and hold up under even just a little bit of failure, let's get back to work!

When I was working at the University of Missouri, I worked a lot with fraternity guys, acting as a mentor and helping set them up for success in the future. We'd talk about how to become men - how to develop as leaders, develop our faith, responsibility, courage, etc. I'd get groups together once a week to sit around and talk about these ideas through books and articles. No matter what group of guys I was with, there was always one week's topic that I enjoyed discussing the most; Failure Week.

I'd get to sit with a bunch of guys who, honestly, were pretty afraid of failure. Some were probably in that fraternity or school because they were afraid of failing at a different fraternity or in a different school. Some lived every day and took every test afraid of failing their parents. And yet there we would find ourselves, breaking down the fear of failure.

One of the things that sticks out to me is a particular Nike commercial clip we'd watch with Michael Jordan.

"I've missed more than 9000 shots in my career. I've lost almost 300 games. 26 times, I've been trusted to take the game winning shot and missed. I've failed over and over and over again in my life. And that is why I succeed."

His Airness said it, not me. I've heard it said before that there is one sure way to succeed faster. The secret? **Fail Faster.**

Chairman and CEO of IMB Thomas Watson once said, "If you want to succeed, double your failure rate."

Yikes. That doesn't sound very fun to me. Failure is pretty tough - every time. Yet, I think he's right on. If you'll focus on failing more you will succeed faster. Make it a competition. If you need to make a certain number of sales a day, see how many rejections you can get in a day. If you are working to get five rejections a day, each one will seem like a small (but ironic) victory. If you have fifty rejections, then I'd bet you got some sales along the way. And if you don't have any wins in those five failures, I'd bet you'll learn from it and get wins the next day. Take this formula to the bank.

Fail more = Succeed more

My Epic Failure

Let me tell you a story of a failure when I started RedWood Recruiting, which is my software company for Greek students. I was excited to get the word out about our new software idea, but I didn't know how to do it. I thought email would be a good method, so I got a list of fraternity advisors' emails from the international office of my fraternity in college.

I didn't know how to go about writing an email, so I just went for it. I wrote up this (apparently) really spammy-sounding email telling them I had a great idea in progress that would greatly help their chapter. I was pumped. I was about to get thirty-five new customers... or so I thought.

I started off by getting three great responses. #Winning. Hook, line, and sinker. I started thinking about that private jet. Then, I got a few emails that were a little more... honest.

"Please cease communication immediately. This is a very unprofessional and disappointing way for you to go about your business."

"I don't know you, and I don't trust you."

"I'm sure your intentions were good; your approach was not."

Then, to make things worse, I got an email from the Executive Director of the fraternity. My stomach dropped. It was a cease and desist letter I was to sign saying that any further communication with the advisors would result in a $100 fine per communication. I signed it, forfeited the email list they had given me, and was back to square one - or maybe even worse.

I was excited to be taking action, to be going after my dreams. I had finally taken some initiative instead of just reading more blogs and more books. I was out in the market, and then it backfired.

So What?

After reeling for an afternoon, I had resolved to stop pursuing the business and shut it down and decided a 9-5 didn't sound so bad after all. But then, fortunately, I sucked it up and realized I had a great learning opportunity in front of me. I could quit on a very good idea that had lots of potential, or I could learn from the mistake and move forward.

Because of that failure, I do things a bit differently now. I've learned. I'm continually working and learning (and still failing) as I cultivate direct marketing channels. I'm better at providing real tangible value to people that subscribe to email updates. Today, I don't have a terrible thirty-five person email list. I have email lists of thousands.

You may look at my mistake and think "what an idiot." But I would take that mindset any day over the mindset of the person who is too afraid of failure to even try. As Chris mentioned in the 20 Mile March, consistent action is the key to success.

Do It Now

I can't emphasize enough the power of doing it now. Tattoo this on your arm: Do. It. Now. When I first started looking into being an entrepreneur for a living, it was so easy to get paralyzed. I would just sit at my computer and read ebook after ebook, blog after blog, and listen to podcast after podcast. I was constantly thinking "Man, that's such a great idea! I totally could have made money doing that! Too bad it's taken." Or I found myself waiting for "the perfect idea" that I could start while I was young and have an early retirement. Guess what? That idea hasn't come for me. I don't know if it will come for a long time - maybe it never will. But I'm not waiting anymore, and neither should you. Stop the excuses and get moving toward your dream, get moving on earning some side income, get moving on whatever it is you know you've wanted to do for a while and just haven't started.

One of the best pieces of advice I can give you is to take action every single day. I have a rule that I try to live by now. When I read/listen to any material on entrepreneurship, I'm not allowed to move on to a second one, until I take some measurable action on my businesses. Without taking action, I will literally spend HOURS absorbing information and then go to bed, no better off than when I woke up. Have you ever found yourself doing this before? You need to become a master at deciding which actions in your life would have the greatest positive impact, and start taking action on them today.

What "Initiative" is Not

When I say "Take action", "Get out there", or "Do it now," I know I'm asking you to take a risk. But I think it's always better to take action and ask for forgiveness later, than to take no action at all because you are waiting for just the right moment. We think you need to trust yourself. If you're reading this book, it's because you have some hopes, dreams and ideas you've been thinking of for a while and haven't taken action on. You want to live a life of freedom. Trust yourself, and go do it.

The other day my co-founder, Brad, and I released Version One of a recent software product. I have been working on it for months. I think it's coming along great, but do I want to release it yet? No way. I see hundreds of things that I can tweak and change about it. I'd love to spend another $5,000 getting it "just perfect" before sending it out into the market, but that's my inner procrastinator talking. What I need to do is launch the product so users can give me real feedback.

So, I launched it and there were some bugs. The first user couldn't even update his profile - one of the most basic functions needed in our software. But we wouldn't have known that had he not tried it and given us feedback. Believe me, I constantly want to keep pushing things back until they are just right, but fellow freedom-fighters, we just can't do that. We have to take initiative. We have to take action.

The Power of Three

As you look back through history, it's interesting to see that humans seem to resonate deeply with the number three. In movies, a three-act structure is the dominant script-writing approach (set-up, conflict, resolution). In storytelling the characters or situations often are in multiples of three (three blind mice, three little pigs, etc). And interestingly enough, when it comes to being a productivity champion, the magic number is no different.

Peter Shallard, an expert in productivity offers an interesting example. In military training, the US has found that grouping things in three is the most effective way to accomplish a task. When teams are assembled with three men and given exactly three tasks to get done, they have the highest rate of success.

Four trainees and three tasks? Less chance of success. Three trainees and two tasks? Not even close.

It's remarkable how the more you look into it the more you see this truth. Our brains love the number three. So what? How does this actually help you? It's going to help you start taking initiative, and has been helping me immensely.

When I wake up, I think through my day. What needs to get done to really count the day as a win? Like Chris, usually my mind floods with ideas; I could really do all sorts of things. If I'm not careful, though, I can get overwhelmed by the many ideas and end up not doing much. I know you've been there before.

What I've been doing to combat this recently has been remarkably effective. I've decided that if I can just complete the three most critical tasks for my day, then I'm the champ. If I don't get to the other tasks, so be it - I can do more tomorrow. All I'm committing to doing is three tasks. I usually get them done pretty efficiently and effectively because my brain doesn't have to worry about anything more than three. It can relax. Then an amazing thing happens for me.

When I get done with the three designated tasks, I don't want to quit. I'm in the zone. I pick three more, and when I get those done, sometimes I pick three more tasks (although sometimes I just watch Kansas State football highlight videos instead). It's amazing. If I would have thought "Dave, you need to get these nine business tasks done today," I probably would have mentally checked out and would have just popped in "Ferris Bueller's Day Off" and called it a day; but because I broke it down in groups of three, I was able to handle it all without being over-loaded. This isn't just my idea either.

AppSumo founder (and employee #30 at Facebook and #4 at Mint) Noah Kagan breaks down what his developer does to stay productive.

He has a master Excel list that lists every single task

that needs to be done, ever. He takes three things each day and puts those at the top. From the beginning of the work day (and he only works 9-5; he doesn't do crazy start-up hours) he does nothing else but get those three things done. No meetings, no phone calls, and no e-mails; his day is focused on the moving forward of three items.

This is something you can start tomorrow. Figure out what three tasks will most impact your life. Write them down and get to work. Your brain will love you for it.

80/20 Rule

Before you decide which three tasks to work on each day, I have to interject the idea of the 80/20 principle into your thinking. This is a fantastic tool that will literally transform your everyday life with little effort.

The principle was first observed by economist Vilfredo Pareto when he saw that 80% of the land in Italy was owned by 20% of the population. He developed the principle further when he observed that 80% of the peas came from 20% of the pea pods in his garden. Since that time, the principle has been widely observed in all sorts of areas of life. 80% of business typically comes from the top 20% of the customers, and 80% of sales are made by the top 20% of sales associates. The 80% of the worlds wealth is owned by the top 20% of the population.

So how do you take this and apply it to your life,

especially when you don't grow peas, own land in Italy, or manage salespeople? The principle applies to all sorts of areas of your life. What you need to do is take some time and find out exactly what you should be spending time on.

First, you need to define the most valuable things in your life. Of everything that you do on a day-to-day basis, what provides the greatest return of value in your life? Who are the people that add the greatest value to your life? What are the activities that you enjoy the most? Those are the aspects of your life that provide 80% of the value in your life. If the principle plays out like I'm arguing it does, then you only do those things with 20% of your waking hours.

For me, I have a few friends and family that really add a lot of value to my life and make me very happy. I have a few activities like basketball and reading that keep me in shape physically and mentally and I love doing. I have a few business activities like calling customers to get feedback and making sales that provide the greatest long term return. And you know what? I don't do all of those things or spend intentional time with those people all that often. I'm guessing it makes up less than 20% of my time. The other 80% is filled with all the other daily activities life brings. I get caught in the busyness.

What's amazing about the power of this principle is that you can double your productivity or double the amount of added value in your life fairly simply. I don't have to start doing the "productive" things 100% of my time. That's too overwhelming for me to think about; I'm just too lazy to be that kind of person. However, if I can start doing the important 20% and do it 40% of the time, that's instantly doubling the very most important things in my life. Wow.

You can also think about it in the reverse. At the risk of sounding a bit cold here, I think it's extremely important to apply what I'm suggesting next. What people, situations, or tasks cause 80% of the frustration, worry, or regret in your life? I'm guessing it's only 20% (and probably less) of your life that causes the most stress. For me, I have had a couple people in my life over the years that have caused almost all of the worry or stress in my life. I decided to stop spending quite as much time with them. I am still their friend, but they aren't as big of a part of my day-to-day life anymore, and it has been amazing how much healthier I am for it. Maybe you need to spend less time in certain places or around certain people. Maybe you need to resolve to spend less time binge-watching Netflix, because you realize it doesn't really leave you happy. Applying the 80/20 in reverse can be amazingly powerful.

An Example From My Life

There are a few tasks in my life that I really hate doing. I am fairly tech-savvy for an amateur, but I have really grown to hate working on some technical problems involved with building websites or various tasks that come along with building a technology business. I can probably figure out a lot of it, but it takes me a long time and puts me in a bad mood. In an effort to remove that stress from my life, I now outsource all of that stuff to places like India and the Philippines.

I recently had to copy and paste over 1000 entries from multiple websites to a database, and while I definitely could have done it, I realized that would have fallen in the 80% stress category for me. I decided the 12-hour project was worth me hiring a guy in Pakistan to do it for $40. That was a powerful application of the Pareto Principle. A few months back I spent several hours really going through every area of my life and figuring out the things I love and the things I hate. Doing that has given me more focus and clarity on what my calling and mission are. I'll keep doing this exercise for years to come.

Take some time now to write down the few things in your life from which you gain the most value. Do those few things more. Also, take some time to write down the few things that stress you out the most. Start doing them less, and delegate what you can. You'll be a noticeably happier person right away. I guarantee it.

Action Step:

Think through your day tomorrow and write down the tasks that need completing in order to consider the day successful. Write those down on a notecard or in your phone. Focus on completing just those three, and let the rest of the day worry about itself.

CHAPTER SEVEN

DON'T BE THE "NETWORKING GUY"

Up until this very second in your life, most of what you have done is not because of *what* you know, but because of *who* you know. Whatever goal of abundance you've had in your mind up till this point will happen primarily on the backs of the network around you. Big, strong network? You can reach a big, strong, successful goal. Small, weak network? You'll get a small, weak, probably-not-going-to-happen goal.

One of the first times I had ever really thought about intentionally deciding who I would be around was when I was twenty and a sophomore in college. I was sitting there listening to Brandon, a speaker and friend of mine. He was going on and on telling these stories of how nuts his high school friends were. One of his buddies had taken a lighter and aerosol spray into a locker room and started torching the outside of the lockers. Well, what he didn't realize was the flame would reach all of the clothes inside of the lockers, which were, well… locked. He almost burned the school to the ground as he watched the clothes inside combust.

At this point in the slew of shock-and-awe stories he had us take out a notecard and write down one single line which I still remember today.

"Show me your friends,

and I'll show you your future"

That's when it clicked. I should carefully decide who are going to be the biggest influencers in my life. I can design my life in such a way that the quality of my network will uphold and even catapult me on to greater and greater things. I've heard it said that you are the average of the five people you spend the most time with. Right now in my life, I get pretty excited about that. I'd love to be the average of the men I'm currently sur-rounded by. But for many of you, that may be an unap-pealing idea. It may be time to get around some new people. Fortunately for Brandon, he realized this prin-ciple and started bringing some different friends into his life, even though they didn't have nearly as many good stories...

The Joy of Connectedness

It's easy when talking about networking for it to feel very cold and impersonal. To be honest with you, I think most people settle for a fairly cold and impersonal life, regardless of how strong their network is. So before we get into the meat of how to build a network, I want to establish an important foundation. A few months back I was sitting down with a friend of mine named Gerard. He told me that one of the greatest decisions in his forty-plus years on earth was to commit to build lasting friendships. When he was in his twenties, he was talking with a group of guys his age. They brought up the idea that they didn't want to change friends every five years like they saw older people do throughout life. They wanted to build really deep friendships. Not just built on golf and business, but on vulnerability, honesty, love, and openness. They wanted to break down the walls of fear that kept people hiding - the walls everyone puts up when they are scared about people really knowing what they are like.

I thought it sounded like a really great plan. Be really, really honest with a few close friends. Be honest to the point that it's painful and terrifying of what they will say or think, and then watch what happens. I've gotten better at making this a practice over the last several years. I have a few friends in my life that I try and tell all of the really embarrassing stuff that I'm ashamed of. I've gotten much better at it, but each time I do it, everything in my mind screams "Don't tell them that! They are going to think you're a total weirdo and stop being your friend. This one has to stay here." It's unbelievably scary, but each time I do it, a remarkable thing happens. They listen, and they respond in love. They let their wall down and sometimes share similar experiences, and sometimes share new ones with me. It takes our friendship to whole new levels - and it always pays off. You really should try it.

I say this to remind you, and remind myself, that no matter how many people you may know, real happiness comes when some of those people really know us. Total transparency is key - not with everyone, but definitely with a few people. Keep that in mind as we talk about building a network. We want to build lifelong friendships with people, not just cold, impersonal teammates.

When it comes to building friendships I always just thought, "I like who I like and if they like me back, then I guess we'll be friends." That's how it works, right? Well, that's one way. I think you'll also realize that you can like a lot of people and a lot of people can like you. You can even keep all of the same friends you have, but if you are someone who is serious about getting Beyond The Grind, you'll add some strategic partners to your network that should positively influence you more than the people around you that may drag you down. In short, you need a better network.

You might think, "I just don't know that many peo-ple," or, "I don't have a very strong network because my parents don't do this or that," etc. Some people have a naturally stronger network than others, but a lack of natu-ral network can be overcome. Many of the most connected people you know have done it from scratch. Don't leave it to chance or who you happen to run in to. Remember, successful people take initiative. Do you want a thriving, life-changing, successful network? Make a plan.

My Personal Network

I really like the idea of expanding my network of friends, and because of that I have a fairly large and diverse group of teammates that support me. I've had some pretty cool opportunities open up, not because of who I am, but because of who I know. Here's a list of a few recent experiences I've had solely from the generosity of my network:

- Stayed a week in Cape Town for free with a wonderful family in an amazing home, even though I had never met them.

- Called my mom a few weeks ago telling her I was standing next to the Dalai Lama, and had met several other famous people that day.

- Was offered free Nebraska football tickets by a friend I met in Peru months before.

- Showed up in Dallas to a K-state bowl game with no tickets, yet got free tickets on the 30 yard line right before kickoff.

- Received $4,500 from friends and family to fund the creation of this book.

- Have multiple job opportunities I could take at a

moments notice.

I don't say any of those things to brag or make myself sound cool. Quite the opposite. I say this to show that a pretty average guy like me can do some really cool things through the strength of my network. Let me show you how you can get lots of awesome people in your network as well.

The Personal Networking Plan

Step 1 - Write Down What You Want

You need to decide what it is you want in life. Really define it. Where are you headed? What is your goal? When I was 24, I wrote this goal out on a notecard, kept it next to my bed and read it out loud every single night:

"By the age of 30, be financially free through starting multiple businesses and creating passive income streams"

- I decided what I wanted - financial freedom.

- I decided when I wanted it - age 30.

- I decided how I would get it - starting multiple profitable businesses.

- I made a final specification - I wanted it to be (relatively) passive income, meaning I didn't want to just be trading time for money anymore.

- I signed it. I made a contract with myself.

- I dated it. (Dad always said documents weren't real until they were dated)

Reminding myself of my goal each night launched my life on a very different trajectory from where it had been headed. I've always been an entrepreneurial-minded guy; but when I actually defined what I wanted, things began to fall into place, and I gained a focused direction on that goal. There is something unbelievably powerful about a clearly defined goal, particularly one that is written down and regularly visited. You'll find yourself and your life moving toward the fulfillment of that goal almost unconsciously.

Shortly after I wrote that goal down I was at a wedding and ran into an old friend whom I hadn't seen in a while. We found ourselves eating hors d'oeuvres when he told me he had quit his job and had been working on starting a software company over the last few months.

I like talking business and all, but normally I would have asked a few good questions about what he was doing with the software stuff and then started yapping about my life. Yet, as he described his career change, my goal popped back into the front of my mind: By age 30 be financially free through starting multiple companies and creating passive income streams. I had been wanting to get into business, but didn't know how.

Because my goal was clearly defined, and I was convinced of my pursuit of it, the conversation hooked me. After getting all the details on how he got started, I had an idea for a software solution of my own a few days later. Soon after that, I had a prototype fully designed on my computer. Nine months later, I had a software product built and my first company, RedWood Recruiting, was off and running. It all started with the clearly defined goal which allowed me to start building my strategic network - the first valuable contact was the guy at that wedding - who also happens to be my co-author, Chris Hull!

Something special happens when you write goals down. You will deeply desire to align who you are with who you want to become. Don't leave this to chance.

Action Step:

Think about what you really want in life. Write it out on a notecard. Be specific enough to give direction. Write the date on it and sign it. You've just made a contract with yourself, effectively doubled your chances of successfully reaching that goal.

Step 2 - Write Down Who Can Help You Get There

After clearly defining what you want, think through all the people that you know that could help you reach that goal. I don't care how well you know them - they are fair game. Make a list of eight people that you know relatively well who can most help you achieve your dream. Eight of them. No more. No less.

A big change would happen in your life if you began to focus your time on building relationships with these eight people. However, your goal should not be to discover how they can help *you*. Instead, focus on how you can help *them*. That's how real networks are built - by giving value instead of taking it. One of my greatest goals in life over the last few years has been to become someone who is a value-giver and not just a value-taker in my relationships. Growing up, I constantly thought about interactions with people through the lens of "What can I get out of this?" In the last several years, various influences in my life have helped me to think more and more about how I can help someone more than how they can help me. People love it, and so do I.

As Keith Ferrazzi, author of Never Eat Alone and master networker says, "The real currency of networking is not greed, but generosity." This mindset shift will absolutely change your life. In fact, I want you to say it out loud right now. If you're at Starbucks or somewhere public, well then say it under your breath, but I need you to say it out loud.

"From now on I, _____, will strive to be a value-giver and not just a value-taker."

Let's get back to the list of eight people you wrote down. Hopefully this is mostly a list of accomplished, established people in your life. You're probably thinking, "What do I even have to offer them of value? I have nothing!"

Several examples might help illuminate this process:

- If you see that they did something important in the newspaper, clip it out, laminate it, and mail it to them. (This one is a little old-fashioned, but my dad is the king of it.)

- Write them a thank you note telling them what an influence they've been in your life. This works even if they only played a small part. They'll appreciate it. (One time I did this and included a gift card for a cup of coffee.)

- Refer business to them. If you do refer someone, call them first to let them know someone is coming their way. Even if it's a voicemail just say, "Hey Mr. Griswald, I just wanted to give you a heads-up that one of my friends will be coming by your place here in the future. I thought you guys might be a good fit to do some business."

- Give them a shout and offer to babysit their kids if they ever need it.

- Call them up and offer to take their kids to a baseball game or some other activity they may enjoy. Believe me, when you love someone's kids, they will love you.

Recently, I sat down with John Hall, an amazing guy and CEO of Influence & Co. I really had one question for him. "How can an average guy like me help hot shots like you?"

John gave me four great social media ideas that you could do today for successful people who have an online presence.

- If they tweet, reply on twitter and engage in a meaningful conversation, helping them increase engagement and reach a wider audience.

- If they tweet something, then retweet it.

- If they post something on LinkedIn - leave a comment or share their post.

- If they have a blog, ask questions on it - be an engaging audience. They will notice and appreciate you for it.

Those are a few practical ways to get you thinking in the right direction. It isn't about being a suck-up or just doing nice things now so you can get what you want later. I've found that when your mindset genuinely shifts from being a taker to a giver, your relationships truly do expand, and you'll find yourself adding value just because you care about people. That's a big life win.

Step 3 - Time to Get Crazy

Now it's time to round out your top ten. (Remember, you only have eight so far.) I want you to list two people that you want to get to know in the next year, but I want the two people to be a bit different. For the first person, write down someone that is just a bit outside of your current personal networks. Maybe he/she is one of your parents' friends. Maybe he is a professor at your college. She should be someone that can help you, but someone you couldn't currently call on for a favor. You may know her, but she may not really know you. Think about that person, then write that name down.

For the second person, I really want to stretch you in your networking mindset. You probably haven't ever thought of doing what I'm about to ask you to do. You probably think it is for "other people" or impossible. I assure you that it is very possible. I want you to write down someone that is famous. This person doesn't have to be famous to everyone, just famous to you. Maybe he is a big name in a particular niche you want to excel in. Maybe she is a big name to everyone you know. Maybe it's J-Lo. Whoever it is, make it someone you would never think about reaching out to - someone outside of your comfortable reach.

How To Reach Them Via Email

Email is most likely going to be the best way to reach this "unreachable" person. It's quick, to the point, and allows them to reply easily. Let's walk through an example of a recent interaction I had with someone that is well known in entrepreneurial circles with whom I wanted to connect.

The person I wanted to reach out to was a guy named Peter Shallard. Peter is known as "The Shrink For Entrepreneurs" and works with a lot of top-tier entrepreneurs helping them get through obstacles and achieve success in their lives. I heard an interview by him on a well-known podcast, and I was instantly hooked. I wanted to reach out to him, so I took my best shot. Here's my email:

"Hey Peter,

Just listened to your interview with Andy at the Foundation, and I'm pumped up! Just started full-time entrepreneurship a few months back and loving it.

Quick question: Are there other solid communities you'd recommen me checking out other than the Fondation and Mixergy?

Those are kind of my circles right now. Thanks Brother. Let me know if a guy from Washington DC can ever do anything for you.

-Dave Rogenmoser"

1. **Subject line:** You want to have a subject line that is short, not spammy, makes them interested, and shows that you have some connection with them already through another avenue. Being endearing doesn't hurt either. Mine was "Foundation podcast-loved it!"

2. **Keep It Short:** Did I want to tell Peter a lot more in this email? Yes. Did I want to explain to him all the problems I was having and get all of his wisdom on how to overcome them? Yes. But that wouldn't have gotten a response. (Plus, it would have been kind of weird.)

   • Let him know how you know him. I heard his podcast on entrepreneurship. I'm an entrepreneur. That's why I'm reaching out. Peter, meet Dave. Dave, this is Peter.

   • Your question. You need to pick one short and relevant question they can be useful in. This should be something they can answer quickly and off the top of their head. Don't make them ask around or research something.

   • Closing line. I wanted to provide a bit of value to him if I could, so I let him know where I lived and told him I'd be down to help him if I could. He knows that's an open door if he needs it.

3. **White Space:** In the body of your email, white

space is your friend. That's a basic rule of copywriting, which is the art of crafting words for persuasion. You probably want each "paragraph" to be one line only (your English teachers are hating me right now) with blank space in between. It's much easier on the eyes to see blank space. When they open it they won't feel overwhelmed by your big monstrous block of text. I sent that email one night and less than twelve hours later I had a response from him waiting in my inbox!

"Heya Dave!

Great to hear from you - I love my Foundation family. Had a blast at the live event last month too!

Solid communities? Oh heck yea, there are a ton. Tell me a bit about where you're at with your business and what you need help with and I will make some recommendations. I'm a connoisseur of fine entrepreneurial communities and I'm glad you asked!

Peter Shallard"

Pretty great response, huh? That guy is awesome. This response led to a nine email conversation that was extremely helpful to my growth as an entrepreneur and gave me one great connection down the road. I'm looking forward to bumping into him in person later on to see how I can help him in any way.

So you see, it isn't that hard to reach out to the "unreachable" people. Even if you do get shut down, what do you have to lose? You never would have known them anyway, so go for it!

My Time With Harvey

The other day, I was talking to one of the most successful businessmen I know. Let's say his name is Harvey Specter. He is a great guy whom I respect a lot. Harvey knows everyone, which is a big key to his success. The thing I can't get my head around is that he doesn't even care about "networking." He's not some politician walking around glad-handing everyone and handing out business cards. In fact, he told me he hates that stuff. So how does Harvey know everyone and have such a strong network? I asked him just that. Here's his big secret on building a powerfully connected network - **He does activities he likes with people he likes.**

That's it. He was talking about how he likes golf a lot so he played in a golf tournament at the local country club and was paired with three young businessmen (including one Big 12 championship linebacker) and here's what he told me.

"Dave, business doesn't always happen on the golf course, but *a lot* of connections happen during a round of 18. I didn't talk business with these guys, but we had a great time together. I can guarantee you that I have three new business connections if I ever need them."

Harvey builds friendships, not cold, impersonal networks. He also loves hunting, so what does he do? He takes big, awesome hunting trips and invites all his friends to go with him. Sometimes they invite their friends along as well, so his network grows over freshly caught fish and big-game stories. Harvey told me of my time in my fraternity, "Dave, in your fraternity, you didn't get 80 best friends, but you did get 80 new teammates." I had never thought of it like that. I made a few best friends for sure, but hadn't realized that the value of my college fraternity network isn't measured by the strength of my close ties, but of my weak ties. That's what separates Harvey's mentality from most.

Most folks think only of the people they are really close to. This guy thinks in terms of extended teams. He's always willing to build a new friendship, not because he wants their stuff, but because he likes friends. Novel idea, isn't it? When we're looking to connect with people we like and people that we can be generous with, we'll watch our networks explode.

I challenge you to be intentional about building your network from here on out. When you meet someone, I challenge you to follow up with them a few days later and ask how you can help them out. I challenge you to focus on building meaningful relationships that could be life-long friends and allies, not just people whose stuff you want. When you are willing to be a person like this, I promise you that you'll enjoy the fruits of a large network of relationships in your life. And you'll be that much closer to living Beyond The Grind.

PART 2

TOOLS TO USE BEYOND
THE GRIND

In the final three chapters, we're going to give you solid, actionable how-to guides for using tools and methods that we think make life Beyond the Grind a lot more fun. We'll teach you exactly how you can:

1. Travel the world for free

2. Outsource your daily tasks overseas

3. Run a Kickstarter campaign to fund and launch your dreams

We've found these to be extremely helpful in-creating a lifestyle that we love, but they aren't for everyone. Some people think the following ideas are a little out there. Maybe they are right, but I'll let you be the judge.

Enjoy.

CHAPTER EIGHT

TRAVEL HACKING 101

Traveling The World For Free

The other day, after many hours of research and very tedious planning, my roommate Matt and I booked an award flight that consists of 25,000 miles in the air. It takes us from DC to Hong Kong to Thailand to Vietnam. Then we go from Bangkok to South Africa, and back to DC. A flight like this may cost about $4000-5000 retail cost, but we booked it for only 80,000 United Award Miles. That's just a few more points than you can get from signing up for one credit card.

When booking this flight over the phone we got transferred to a "higher up" for United who laughed when he saw what we wanted to do for 80k miles and said it was "impossible, man. It'll cost you 200,000 miles to do something like that."

Well, stay tuned, ladies and gentlemen, because we're going to show you how we booked the impossible, and how you can too!

Note: The strategies of accumulating airline miles can change quickly. The below is true at the time of this writing. Please do your own research or contact me to learn about new techniques. Also, please note that the credit card strategies outlined here are mostly only available in the US.

Travel Hacking

A while back I heard the phrase "travel hacking" thrown out by a friend. Most people are probably turned off by the word "hacking," but I was ridiculously interested. As I looked more into what "travel hacking" was, it had much less to do with "hacking" and much more to do with legally and ethically getting free trips to pretty much anywhere in the world, staying at crazy nice hotels, and tapping into the great benefits freely provided by credit card companies, yet rarely taken advantage of by regular Joe's like you and me.

So I did some research online, applied for five different credit cards (yikes), and utilized a few techniques to meet the minimum spending requirements given by the credit card companies. Within a month, I had earned a little over 235,000 hotel and airline points. The thing is, I did most of that in a week before spending the other three weeks in Peru, traveling and not thinking about credit cards at all.

To put 235,000 points in perspective, in probably

10-15 total hours time, I earned two free round-trip business class tickets to Europe, a free round-trip domestic flight to anywhere in the US, a free stay at a 5-star hotel, and **nine** free nights at Club Carlson Hotels.

I'm literally sitting here smiling thinking about all the great adventures and trips ahead that are now possible because of these rewards. I am doing it, and you can do it too. Before I give you a step by step guide, here's the answers to a few questions I get a lot.

Is 'travel hacking' even legal?

That's the first question that popped into my head, and to answer it clearly - the answer is YES. What I and almost all people who are using credit cards to earn rewards are doing is totally and completely legal. It is just a process maximizing the available credit card rewards program.

Is 'travel hacking' time-consuming?

Most people don't have much time to spend and neither do I. I'd rather be experiencing life than frittering it away earning little reward points here and there. I'm going to teach you to apply the 80/20 rule to your rewards points earnings. 80% of the reward points can be earned using 20% of the time. The level of rewards-earning I'm going to teach you will take a few hours a week, or even less.

How difficult is 'travel hacking'?

That's a difficult question to answer, because there are so many different "levels" of it. Some of the most extreme travel hackers I've met online pretty much do it full-time. Have you seen the show "Extreme Couponing" where these ladies spend their entire lives clipping and using coupons? Their life isn't what I want, but it also doesn't deter me from using the occasional coupon. I don't want you to become an "extreme travel hacker," so I'm going to give you the basics to simplify the idea in your mind and let you decide how much you'd like to do.

Who should avoid 'travel hacking'?

If you already have trouble with credit cards, and debt in general, don't step into the credit card reward world. Seriously, put the book down, walk away, and start paying down that debt. This isn't for you.

Also, because it is difficult to know exactly how banks will view the application of multiple credit cards, if you are going to take out a big loan for a house, boat, etc in the next 1-2 years, I wouldn't engage in this practice. That's not to say this isn't very safe, but I don't want to be the one that gets you a little bit more expensive loan on your house. That could cost you lots down the road.

Won't 'travel hacking' ruin my credit score?

This is maybe the most common question I get. The answer is no. In the short run, when you apply for a credit card, you receive what's called a 'hard inquiry' on your credit report. This has very little effect on your score, but you may see your score drop a few points. But don't worry, this will be offset after a few months and you'll actually see your credit score go up even above your previous score.

This is due to multiple factors that I won't get fully into in this book, but factors such as "credit line utilization" percentage (the percentage of your total available credit that you currently use) and length of credit history (the average age of your different credit cards or other lines of credit) will start to help your credit score.

How do I check my credit report?

While it isn't free to get your credit score, you are allowed by the government to get your credit report for free each year. Before we get started, I highly recommend doing so. You can do this by going to www.annualcreditreport.com. It is very helpful to see your credit report, especially before beginning to apply for any credit cards. I suggest you do it every single year.

When I first started applying for cards, I got declined for one. I didn't know why. My credit score was over 700, and I had paid every single bill on time. I got a letter in the mail a few days later that told me why.

Your credit report shows a delinquent account.

What the heck? I had no idea what it was talking about - I didn't have any delinquent accounts that I knew about. So I got on and looked at my credit report for the first time.

Sure enough, there was a three-year-old account that showed I owed the city of Columbia, MO $541 for utilities that never got shut off after I moved out. I thought I had cleared all of that up years ago, but it was still unresolved and hurting my credit score and my ability to use credit to my advantage. I got the matter settled quickly and easily; I just wish I had checked my credit report first.

How do I find out my credit score?

There are a number of ways to get your credit score online by paying a small fee. These can change frequently, so I won't get into specifics on the paid versions, but a quick google search will give you results.

The free method I use to get my credit score is a service and iPhone app called Credit Karma. It shows you your Transunion credit score, which is one of three different credit scores that you have. The other two credit scores you get are from Equifax and Experian.

Credit Karma gives you monitoring of your credit score and updates once a week. It will also give you advice and tips on what cards to apply for, how certain actions will affect your credit score, and many more tips. I recommend downloading Credit Karma ASAP. It's easy and free.

Ok, I'm ready! How exactly do I do this?

Ok so you think you'd like to make these travel dreams happen, you feel good about the above questions, and you're ready to get started. So what do you do? Let's get into it. I'm going to explain what I call the first two 'levels' of travel hacking.

Most of you should start taking advantage of the rewards available by utilizing level one. This is easy, hard to mess up, and will get you some good rewards pretty quickly.

The second level is a little bit more complicated, but if you have the time and willingness to learn, this is going to get you points at a very high rate. You'll be taking sweet trips anywhere in the world in a few months. I guarantee it.

There are deeper levels of travel hacking as well, but we won't get into those here. I just want to teach you the basics. Again, I recommend starting slowly. Then, as you feel comfortable and understand the basic principles, you can ramp it up later.

Level 1

Level one involves figuring out how much you normally spend each month and applying for 1-2 high-reward credit cards every 3-6 months. Then you simply put all of your normal spending onto those credit cards and reach the minimum spending requirements naturally.

What do I mean by "minimum spending requirements?" Rewards credit cards have unusually high introductory offers to get people to sign up and start using their credit cards. Right now, the Chase Sapphire Preferred Card offers you 40,000 award points if you sign up and spend $3,000 on their credit card in the next 3 months. 40,000 points is a ton, considering it would normally take you spending about $40,000 to get the same amount. So taking advantage of these offers can be very lucrative.

Step by Step

Step 1: Find out your total monthly expenses, but don't factor in your spending that can't easily be put on a credit card. More experienced people can easily pay for everything using credit cards, including mortgages, but for level 1, we're not going to worry about that.

Let's say you spend $2,000 a month in expenses that you could put on a credit card. That's your baseline for how many credit cards you can safely apply for and still reach the minimum spending requirements. Most credit cards require you to spend their minimum spend limit in 3 months. So in three months you can spend $6,000 on a credit card.

Step 2: Research which credit cards have high rewards and low minimum spending requirements. These change frequently, but at the time of this writing, here are some specific examples.

The Chase Sapphire Preferred card is my go-to card to recommend to newcomers at the time of this writing. Is it always the best for all people in all situations? No. Is it going to be a really really good card for everyone regardless of their situation? Yes. This is one you want in your wallet.

Chase Sapphire: Minimum spending - $3,000 in three months

Rewards - 40,000 Chase Points (Called Ultimate Rewards)

So, if you apply for that one and get approved, you can find another $3,000 worth of minimum spending requirements and be right at your three month spending total.

Another great card for everyone is the Barclay Arrival Plus World Elite MasterCard. They give you 40,000 miles after spending $3,000 in the first three months. That can be redeemed for $440 in travel.

To summarize, if you applied for both of those cards

and got accepted, you would spend the next three months putting all of your normal spending on these two cards. After spending $6,000 on them, you'd have about $1,200 worth of travel spending at your fingertips. Not bad for doing nothing besides changing out two pieces of plastic in your wallet? **Note:** Technically the Sapphire isn't plastic but is a metal card and yes, it makes you feel like a boss when you use a metal card.

Level 2

Level 2 is for folks who:

- Want to travel a lot and sit in Business andFirst-class when possible.

- Don't spend much money normally, so it would be hard to reach minimum spending requirements.

- Have a bit of free time, think this stuff is a ton of fun, and want to get tons of free travel, all while increasing their credit score.

- Are a little bit adventurous.

If the above is you, then let's dive into level 2. But to do so, I need to introduce you to the world of manufactured spending.

Manufactured spending happens when you use your credit card to purchase cash equivalents (typically Visa gift cards, but also many other options) and then use them to pay off your credit card bill. So in the end, you can reach higher minimum spending requirements and it doesn't cost you much to do it.

Sound confusing? Let's talk specific ways to do this.

1) Walmart BlueBird Account

The bluebird account is basically a Walmart debit card. You can load money onto it using a Visa Gift Card (VGC) and then use it to pay off your credit card bill.

Step By Step

A. Go to bluebird.com and sign up for a free account. They will send you a Bluebird card in the mail in 7-10 days. Alternatively, you can buy a Bluebird card at a Walmart store, but it will cost you $5. Keep your $5 and get one online now.

B. You need to find a store that lets you buy Visa Gift Cards using your credit card. I specifically say Visa because they have a PIN number associated with them and that's key. If you buy an American Express gift card, you won't be able to use it to load your bluebird account.

I recommend going to CVS (this may change) or any number of grocery stores to buy your Visa Gift Cards. I typically buy the $500 cards, because there is generally a $6.95 fee that you pay when you buy them. If you buy $500 the fee is only 1.4% of the card's value. However, at first you might consider buying a card for $100 if that makes you more comfortable. Sometimes $200 is the maximum value card available for purchase.

C. Once you have a Visa Gift Card(s), head to your nearest Walmart with your gift card(s) and your Bluebird card. You can load it onto your bluebird card two different ways.

You can go up to a cashier and say "I'd like to load money onto this Bluebird card." You'll then hand them the Bluebird card and when the cashier is ready, you can swipe your VGC which acts exactly like a debit card. The PIN number on the cards are typically the last 4 digits of the card.

After entering the amount you'd like to transfer, the transaction should complete, and you will have success-fully emptied your VGC onto your bluebird account.

OR

You can go to the Walmart Money Center ATM machine and load it there. This is my preferred method, though sometimes the machine is sketchy and doesn't work properly. It's pretty self-explanatory once you get to the machine. When you're at the ATM, hit "Bluebird" button and follow the steps to load your Bluebird account.

Note: You can only load $1,000 per day and $5,000 per month onto your bluebird account.

D. Once you've loaded your Bluebird card with money, you can link it to your credit card account via the Bluebird website. This is pretty simple. Now, just hop online and pay off the credit card bill you built up from buying the gift cards!

How Much Spending You Can Manufacture

Let's say you spend $1,000/mo on regular living expenses and can put all of that on a credit card. Plus you go to Walmart five different days a month and deposit $1,000 into your bluebird account each time. At the end of that month, you would have successfully spent $6,000 on your credit card. That's a lot of extra spending toward minimum spending requirements!

What rewards can you receive from $6,000 in minimum spending requirements? Without getting too specific, because deals change all the time, let's look at the example in level 1 again. For $6,000 in three months you could get about $1,200 in travel. You could do all of that in one month, and then get $1,200 each in month 2 and in month 3.

If you played your cards right and had cards that transferred to United, you could use 160,000 miles to take a first class trip to India, which would cost about $12,000 if you didn't have reward points. Bada bing, bada boom. That's not a bad life.

Now, how much does it really cost to do that?

If you buy 10 $500 VGC's to load $5,000 onto your Bluebird account and each one has a $6.95 fee, then you'll spend $69.50 on the gift cards. Plus add in the cost of your time to go to CVS (or other grocery stores) a few times and Walmart five times. Then add the cost of gas to drive around to these places. While manufactured spending is very cheap, it's not free and can be a bit time-consuming.

You'll need to decide for yourself if it's worth it to you. I'd definitely recommend starting slowly and using the principles described above even if you use different methods or the methods change.

The Trip Around The World for 80k miles

To open this chapter I mentioned how we booked a massive reward flight using United miles we accumulated from the above techniques. Without going incredibly in-depth on how we booked our flight, I'll show you the principles we used and how you can use them too. You've done the above work of accumulating the miles, now let's get you your flights.

When I first wrote out this section, it was incredibly

detailed on exactly how we booked this crazy itinerary. It mentioned all sorts of weird loopholes and complicated processes that took us hours to learn. Then I realized "Man, this isn't very helpful." If you would like to know all the ins and outs of this, feel free to reach out to me to discuss more - but for the purposes of being helpful - I've decided to just write about the basics here.

The Rules

United has several rules that you need to work within when booking an award flight. I won't go into all of them, but will describe the ones involved in an international round-trip flight.

1. You are allowed one stopover (explained below).

2. You are allowed two open-jaws (explained below).

3. If you land in a location and stay for less than 24 hours, it is considered a long layover, and not a stopover.

Here's how you can use the above rules to your benefit and make your trip a little cooler. Let's say you want to visit Rome and travel Italy for a week. Typically, you would just book a round-trip flight to Rome. Straight there, straight home. That's fine for some people, but we're trying to sell books here, so let's spice that trip up a little bit and add in some free stuff.

The Stopover (not available on domestic flights)

A free stopover means you can land somewhere either on the way to or the way from your destination and hang out as long as you want (up to a year). This is awesome because it lets you visit somewhere that you weren't even really intending on seeing. For our above flight, we were headed to Vietnam as our destination, but wanted to visit somewhere cool on the way home. In this case, South Africa became our stopover where we spend 6 days.

So, in the scenario where you are heading to Rome for a week, maybe you would like to see Madrid if possible. Well, it certainly is possible! You can stop in Madrid on the way there or on the way back for free. Just add it to your itinerary.

Two Open-Jaws (not available on domestic flights)

An open-jaw happens when you land at one airport and leave from a different airport. For example, you can land in Madrid, take a week to travel around Spain and over to Barcelona by train, and then fly from Barcelona to Rome. In this situation, Madrid would be your stopover, the open-jaw would be the segment in between Madrid and Barcelona, and Rome would be your destination.

23-Hour Layovers (not available on domestic flights)

23 hour layovers are best used when you would land in a city for a quick plane change, but instead of having a layover of a few hours, you can move your connecting flight back to the next day and spend a day visiting the city, provided it is not longer than a 24-hour layover. For example, when booking your flight from Barcelona, you might notice that you have a 2 hour layover in Paris. "Wow," you think, "I'd sure love to see Paris if I could." Well, there's good news for you.

You can't use your stopover to visit Paris, because you already used it to see Madrid, but you could use a 23-hour layover. In this case, you would see that your flight lands at 6:00 pm in Paris. You could then look to see if there was a one way flight from Paris to Rome departing the next day. As long as it was departing before 6:00 pm, you could take it. So you could board the 4:30 pm flight and get to spend 22.5 hours in Paris. It's not a ton of time, and it doesn't work real well in some cities (like London) because the airport might be too far from the city to make it worth your while, but for a lot of cities, this is a fun way to see someplace new.

So we just took a flight that initially looked like this: (note: these are not actual routes, but examples to get the idea across)

1. Chicago-Rome

2. Rome-Chicago

Price: 80,000 United Mileage Plus Miles

And turned it into this:

1. Chicago-Madrid (Stop-over)

2. Madrid to Barcelona by train (Open Jaw)

3. Barcelona-Paris (23 hour layover)

4. Paris to Rome

5. Rome-Chicago

Price: 80,000 United Mileage Plus Miles

This chapter is meant to be a primer on Travel Hacking and Manufactured Spending. This is not an exhaustive guide. You could do so much more research on it and I could share so many more details, but I tried to make it as basic and applicable as I could. I am not responsible for any of your actions as a result of this chapter. Use these techniques at your own risk.

A great resource for more information is the message board at www.flyertalk.com. Those guys really love this stuff, and a lot of them get over a million miles a year and manufacture spending of over 20k per month. Shoot me an email with questions or success stories you have. We'd love to hear about folks out there reaching some of their travel dreams!

Again, many of these methods listed above are subject to frequent change. I would do a quick Google search or email us with questions about the current methods available. It's an ever-changing game, but we think that's part of the fun!

Like an good adventure? To watch the video of us eating a live King Cobra on this trip, head over to getbeyondthegrind.com/80ktrip

CHAPTER NINE

LIVING THE OUTSOURCED LIFE

Personal Overseas Outsourcing - Virtual Assistants

Do you spend a lot of your time doing 'busy work' in your personal life or in the office? Do you find yourself spending too much time doing tasks outside of your strengths, instead of focusing your time and energy on the things that provide you the most value? If you have simple tasks that are taking up your valuable time, then it might be time for you to begin outsourcing a bit of your work overseas for a few dollars an hour. I've started doing this more and more, and in this chapter I'll teach you how to do the same.

We've all heard of the growing ability to outsource work overseas. Typically when we think of outsourcing, we picture products being made overseas by low-cost laborers and sent back over to the US. This is true; product outsourcing has been the largest aspect of outsourcing over the years. But what we're beginning to see more and more in the world is services outsourcing. While typically, services are local in nature, as the expanding use of the internet continues, we're seeing the growth of overseas services impacting our daily lives.

I'd bet that all of the businesses in the Fortune 500 use some facet of services outsourcing to places like India, Indonesia, Philippines, or Pakistan. But what most regular folks like us don't realize is that we can (and probably should) personally outsource parts of our lives to overseas workers or Virtual Assistants.

Time is our greatest resource. It's extremely abundant, yet remarkably limited. We have an hour once, and then we never have it again. I want to help you here consider a few resources that will help you get some of your precious time back.

How I Got Sucked Into This Outsourced World

When starting my first software company, RedWood Recruiting, I needed to hire a software developer to work with us in building our product, but I didn't know anyone who could do it, nor did I know how to find anyone. I was stuck. Through a friend, I heard of a website called odesk.com. According to their Wikipedia page, oDesk is a global online work platform where businesses and independent professionals connect and collaborate remotely.

Basically, Odesk is like Amazon for services instead of products. It is filled with people who do all sorts of skills for all different dollar amounts. From American business consultants charging $150/hr to grow your business, to Indian data entry workers who will organize and copy data to a spreadsheet for $1.50/hr - Odesk has it all.

Remember, I needed some software development done, and Odesk had a plethora of software developers - at least I was in the right ballpark now. I did a bit of research on how to find a freelance developer, and I posted a job on Odesk.

What happened next was not what I was expecting. Within 12 hours, I had over 50 applicants for my job. Amazing! I was stoked. I had 50 highly qualified developers wanting to create my software product, right? Wrong. I had about three qualified developers hidden in a field of 47 people who didn't even really read my job posting, were terribly unqualified for the job, and were only charging $6-10/hr, even though I was looking to hire someone in the $50-70/hr range.

Fortunately, Odesk makes it very easy to sort through all of the candidates and find the diamonds in the rough. After finding a few people that seemed to be a good fit, I began chatting with them more about my product needs and desires. Talking with people from different cultures around the world certainly has its entertaining challenges. One of the first guys I talked to opened the conversation like this:

"How are you doing, dear?"

Not exactly how strangers and potential business partners in America greet each other, but maybe that's how things work in other places.

The second guy I talked to was from Germany. We chatted for over an hour about how to build and create a recruitment software product for fraternities. About an hour in, we just weren't quite connecting on the idea. I couldn't figure out why. Finally, I asked "Hold on. Do you even know what a college fraternity is?" Turns out he had no idea. Major culture gap there that I didn't recognize. My fault.

Finally, I met a sharp guy from the States who just loved programming. We chatted for a bit, discussed the scope and complexity of the project, and after talking with my co-founder, we hired him. He successfully built the first version of our recruitment product, which is making money today. While there have been some communication issues and complications when dealing with someone you've never actually met, we've gotten a great product at a great price. I had gotten a great return for my money, but more than that, a whole new world seemed to open up to me - a world where I could intermittently hire skilled services to help my life.

Most of you aren't looking to create a software product or hire some full time developer - but you can still benefit greatly from outsourcing some of your busy work overseas for a few dollars an hour.

My Second Virtual Employee

I mentioned in an earlier chapter how I needed to copy and paste a list of over 1000 entries from multiple websites into an Excel sheet. Not exactly something I was excited to do. But fortunately for me, it was exactly Shoharab Shamrat's cup of tea! I posted another job on Odesk describing in detail the problem I was looking to solve and what I was willing to pay. After sorting through another huge list of applicants, I found my man, Shoharab, a data entry specialist from Bangladesh. He seemed nice, friendly, could speak decent English, and guaranteed his work. If I wasn't satisfied with his work, I didn't have to pay him. Oh, and he was excited to do it for $1.65 an hour. Win for him, win for me.

I was hoping that he would be able to fully understand the type of information I needed him to gather and be able to go out on the internet, find all the websites I was looking for, and put all the information into a document for me. That wasn't exactly the case. Instead, I had to walk him step-by-step through every stage of the process. I had to tell him exactly which websites to look at, exactly what I wanted the spreadsheet to look like, correct some of the mistakes on the spreadsheet, lather, rinse, repeat.

To be honest, it was a little bit more like working with a machine than it would be like working with a regular employee. But what did I expect? I'll admit, It was kind of a confusing task, plus I was only paying $1.65 per hour.

So after a few back and forth conversations, I received my database filled with thousands of entries. Shoharab was pleasant to work with, and $42 and 27 hours of work later, we both walked away very satisfied with our new business relationship. He was making good money, and I was getting a good service. Second try at outsourcing work was a success, and I'm still working with him today. Shoharab is still with me a year later and now many of my friends use him for various internet tasks - he's up to $3.00/hr!

Do You Have An Atiqur?

My success with Shoharab got me thinking a lot more about what could be done out there. Personally, I had been wanting a personal website set up to act as home-base for all the activities I was involved in, but I had never really wanted to go through all the trouble of figuring it out. Now that I knew I could easily find people who would be interested in setting it up for me, I decided to move forward with the project. I hopped back onto Odesk, where I was now a certified employer, and did a quick search for "WordPress expert." For those of you who don't know, WordPress is the most popular website platform, commonly referred to as a CMS (content management system), in the world. I wanted to build the site using WordPress, but I was not looking forward to setting it all up myself. But, you guessed it, my soon-to-be new friend Atiqur Rahman was more than happy to set up my site! And all for a (very) small fee.

I posted a job again on Odesk, sifted through the 46 applicants and began chatting with Atiqur. I asked if he could get the job done, and what was his response?

"Sure, why not?"

I liked this guy already. After talking for a bit with him about what he could and couldn't do, he got my new personal website up and running. Atiqur is the man. He's invited me over to his home in Bangladesh through this process, and we now talk a bit here and there just about life, WordPress aside. I keep asking him to do various things for me from time to time, and if he can't do it, he puts me in touch with someone who can.

Now You Try

I'm just skimming the surface when it comes to what a virtual personal assistant can do. This is a huge industry that is only going to keep getting bigger, better, and more sophisticated. There are already a bunch of firms popping up that provide reliable virtual assistants to take some work off your hands for a fraction of the cost of an American assistant. So when you're thinking through your own life, a lot of the tasks your personal secretary can do for you, you can start sending overseas.

I'm not saying you should go fire your assistant and tell them Shoharab will be taking his or her place. Keep them on the team. What I am lobbying for is that you start outsourcing some of the busy work you have them do to free them up to help you with more mission-critical work.

Personally, I think we're all going to have virtual assistants someday down the road. It sounds crazy now, but the world is getting smaller and it's just becoming way too easy to bring someone onboard to help me organize email, schedule appointments, and edit my photos. I haven't moved to getting a full-time dedicated assistant just yet, but I hope to be doing that in the near future!

If you're interested in outsourcing a bit of work, but aren't yet sold on the idea about someone outside of the US working on the team, you might consider using a slick service called Zirtual.com. They have a great website where they help you connect with US based virtual assistants who will still be less than hiring a full-time assistant, but can help you when needed on research, scheduling, or any number of tasks. Check them out!

I know the idea of outsourcing some of your life, especially internationally can be a bit outside the box for most of you. That's okay. If you don't want to do it, that's no problem - it probably isn't for a lot of people right now. My hope is that you will begin to consider ways your life might be better and more freed up through outsourcing, and for you to know that it is an option! If you'd like to talk more about how you can personally get started outsourcing your life, hit us up.

CHAPTER TEN

READY. SET. GO.

Well, we did it folks. We've made it to the end of the book, which strangely feels kind of like the beginning of something new. We hope that we have shaken your life up a bit. We won't be so bold as to think that we've revolutionized your life or anything like that - we're not that smart or interesting. But we do hope that we've put some words to something that maybe you've felt or believed all along, but maybe you had never quite been able to articulate.

We don't plan on this being the end, and neither should you. We'll be coming out with other books here soon, so be sure to follow us. We're serious when we say we want to help, don't be afraid to email us at dave@getbeyondthegrind.com and chris@getbeyondthegrind.com. If you apply what you've just read, take consistent action each and every day, we guarantee that you will live a life that stands out from your peers.

Action Guides:

If you haven't yet, be sure to head over to getbeyondthegrind.com/action to download the free action guide of all the action steps throughout the book. Be the type of person that takes action and head over there!

We'd love your Amazon review!

If you enjoyed our book, please head over to amazon.com and leave us a review. We'll use your feedback for our next book, and your review helps us get the book out there!

Bonus Chapter Ahead: To learn how we used Kickstarter to raise money and get the publishing completely paid for before the book was finished, stick around for the bonus chapter: **How We Used Kickstarter To Launch Our Dreams.**

BONUS CHAPTER

HOW WE USED KICKSTARTER TO LAUNCH OUR DREAMS

When we started Beyond the Grind, we had no idea how to write, publish or market a book. Sometimes we even struggled reading them. How were we even supposed to sell the book? Should we just back a truck up to Barnes and Noble and start setting up a display next to the Moleskin journals? Maybe we needed to email the New York Times and see if they would be so kind as to put us on their fancy book list? We didn't have any idea how to start, but then we stumbled upon what seemed like a fun way to both fund the publishing of the book as well as do the initial marketing to build momentum for the book launch. The idea? We needed to launch a Kickstarter Project.

What A Kickstart Project Is

Kickstarter.com is a crowdfunding platform in which regular folks can get projects of any kind funded and backed by a large number of supporters. It's great because it connects people around great causes and helps ideas get off the ground that would normally stay in a person's head. If you have an idea that you'd like to Kickstart into action, we'd love to help you think through how you can launch your own Kickstarter project.

Our initial Kickstarter goal was to raise $8,000 in order to fund all the publishing costs. Honestly, this was a crazy amount of money in our mind. But after thinking, dreaming, and praying about what amount we would need to fully fund the release of the book, we landed on the daunting goal of 8k.

Next, we had to create the campaign. What did we think the first step to that should be? Naturally, we figured we should make a sick video. That's when we called our good friend Patrick McNamara to bring in the big guns. Patrick owns a photography business, Drawn To The Image, in Annapolis, MD, and has tons of style and great equipment. We knew he would be able to make us look good.

After talking with Patrick, we created the script for the video, outlining everything we wanted to say. It can actually be pretty hard to distill a book with 30,000 words down to a few paragraphs of speech. After we dialed it in, we met up with Patrick for the shoot. About two hours of actual shooting and 15 hours of video editing later, out popped our sweet Kickstarter promo video. This would be the fuel to the Kickstarter fire.

Next, we made a list of a lot of our friends from around the country. We had been fortunate to run in a lot of different circles over the years, so we had a pretty eclectic and expansive network. We thought "Who are some of the movers and shakers in each of these different circles?" If we could reach them and get them on board, we thought the rest of the dominoes would come with it. So we texted each of those people, tracked the responses and made sure to follow up diligently with them. A lot of you reading this got that text. You are awesome - thanks for being a key piece to this dream!

Then we set up an account on Hootsuite - a social media management tool. This would be app in which we would organize all of our accounts - Twitter, Facebook, and LinkedIn. This was really key, because now we could write up one post, and send it to all six of our different accounts in a single click. This would be a huge timesaver in the grand scheme of things. Luckily, we found a free 60-day trial for their "Pro" service, which saved us hundreds of dollars. You can probably still find this by searching online

Once everything was designed and ready to go, it was finally time to put the rubber to the road. We crossed our fingers, got our tweeter machine fired up and clicked "Launch Project."

As with most Kickstarter projects, our first 24 hours was a hit. After the first day, we were on pace to hit 200% of our goal - what was so hard about this Kickstarter stuff? We texted tons of friends and family, posted content to all of our social media outlets, and the ball was rolling. Then day three started, and let's just say that things… flatlined a bit. We had made the assumption that 80% of our pledges would come from people we knew and another 20% would be from people outside of our networks - random people who we sometimes found ourselves referring to as "rando's." After the launch and reaching out to a huge group of people, a lot of our people had been pledging, but where were the rando's? They should have started trickling in after all the retweets our friends had sent out; but they didn't come. After a bit of a slump in days 3-6 we hit the trail hard on day six and went from $1,500 to $2,600 in about 15 hours. Some great folks really put the team on their back.

We had a steady climb from $2,600-$4,200, but ultimately, we just couldn't get it done. We worked hard, reached out to our networks, called in favors, but never got the full traction we needed to hit $8,000. With the ending deadline approaching, we had a decision to make. Throw in the towel, forget about the book, and become professional trash men, OR…. we could restart the Kickstarter at a lower amount. While we really, really hated admitting defeat of the first Kickstarter and looking like we couldn't pull it together in front of all our friends and family, we remembered that failure isn't a bad thing, what's important is how you respond. People would probably benefit more from reading about two chums who couldn't figure out how to run a good Kickstarter, but eventually figured it out, than two guys who nail everything on the first try. We texted all of the first backers and asked them if they would move their pledge over to a new Kickstarter if we launched it. Like total champs, they said they would.

A Phoenix Rises From the Ashes

Restarting a Kickstarter is pretty simple. None of the backers from the first one got charged a dime, because we didn't meet the goal. All we had to do was to copy and paste everything over to a new campaign, hit launch, and then ask everyone to sign on and give again. Because of (but most likely despite) our constant nagging and reminders to friends to hop and re-pledge, we hit our goal of $4,500 on November 19th, 2014. We were pretty much millionaires.

Now without further ado, I present to you the people who funded the movement. We asked them to share a thought on what helps them live Beyond the Grind.

* * *

Andrew Lovell - Realize that your actions can impact people whom you do not know/will never meet. You matter and you CAN exact change. We are a global community and no man, or woman, is an island.

Jimmy Blee - The wisdom I offer is nothing I conjured up on my own, but comes from my God in heaven and is wisdom that has become a life long journey of learning and change: Learn to be thankful, no matter the circumstance whether good or bad; learn to live selflessly; and learn to be humble. These are given to us for fighting opposition, healing old wounds, and building meaningful, long-lasting relationships. These will change your life and the lives of those around you.

Alex Hrebec - Go Cats.

Patty Rogenmoser - Proverbs 3:5-6. "Trust in the Lord with all your heart and lean not on your own understanding; in all your ways acknowledge Him and He will make your paths straight." Align your plans with God's plans for you. Discover your passion and your giftedness and use them. Be others-centered, not self-centered. Follow Jesus. John 10:10 "I have come that they may have life, and have it to the full."

David Lufkin - Love God with all of your heart, mind and soul and love your fellow man as you would yourself.

Nathan Gertson - Imagine a world where we all put aside our small ambitions and dream for Something and Someone greater than the Grind. That dream realized is a world-changing movement.

Robert Flack - There's a good life and a great life out there. The good life is easy, comfortable, but small and self-focused. The Great life is harder, unselfish, requires risk, and impacts eternity. Run after the great life!

John Sarver - True success is love. Give your life towards meeting the needs of others, especially helping people in their need for real relationship with God & with people.

Ben Harvey - To change the world and live 'Beyond the Grind', you must live like never before; live in such a way that others can not or will not live.

David Sabin - "The opportunity for the greatest turnaround in college football exists here today, and it's not one to be taken lightly" - Legendary head football coach Bill Snyder.

Karson Merkel - A wise man once told me, "The right thing at the wrong time is the wrong thing."

John Michael Eplee - "To know is to concede thought."

Cooper Mach - A good tie can make an old suit look new.

AZ Moyer - When you are hunting elephants, don't get distracted chasing rabbits.

Spencer Bontrager - You still have a lot to learn. You still have a lot to see. You still have a lot of people to meet. You still have a lot to do.

Tyler Geisler - Life Beyond the Grind is an idea most will likely miss and few will have the guts to pursue. You need a vision, commitment, passion and purpose for life that is second to none; which will likely be found or crafted from another person. Jesus gave me mine… who will give you yours?

Drew Peters - There is glory in the grind and the grind leads to Glory.

Ethan Marino - "How do you go from where you are to where you wanna be? And I think you have to have an enthusiasm for life. You have to have a dream, a goal. And you have to be willing to work for it." That quote by Coach Jim Valvano has always been one of my favorites. I believe that such enthusiasm comes from the people you surround yourself with. I am grateful to be surrounded by

fsdfsdf friends and family that have always shown me the upmost love and support. Dave is one of those friends, as he has always provided me with guidance and encouragement throughout our friendship. I wish he and Chris the best of luck with their first book, and I hope there are more to come!

Justin D Brownlee - Fellow grinder.

Nathan Sheahan - Simply the idea of this book inspired me to start my own business while in college!

Ethan Sageser - If you have to work, why not find a way to enjoy it and make it a passion.

Nick Hehemann - Matthew 6:33.

Jake Sumner - Be intentional.

Stephen Norman - Always stay positive.

JP Risenhoover - One day your life will flash before your eyes, make sure it is worth watching.

Hank Nelson - Take every thought captive in obedience to Christ. 2 Cor. 10:5

Jordan Brown - Knowing Jesus personally as my Lord and Provider for all things.

John Philip (JP) Morgan - Do you see a man skilled in his work? He will stand before kings; he will not stand before obscure men.

Kyla Krissek - "True happiness... is not attained through self-gratification, but through fidelity to a worthy purpose." Helen Keller

Kyle Mathews - I be on the grind! But when I get off the grind, I move myself beyond it, and this book takes me there and puts me in a position to be successful while I'm there.

Jackie Hull

Rob Ivy

Joseph "Salt" Wilson

Michael Rogenmoser

Matt Kennedy

Tonya Zunigha

Laura McLemore

Brady Reed

Jason Morgan

Kevin Weaver

Brad Schnefke

Alysse Whatley

Anna Ewing

Jonathan & Lauren Hull

Blake & Kelly Howard

Caleb Alexander

Chris Miller

David Gibbens

Cory Riddle

Jason Hoover

Brett Heidebrecht

Nick Ward

Travis Holloway

Stephen Andersen

Larry Lovell

Tyler and Dina Carey

Karen Rose Trifiletti

Collin "Slim" Smith

Dustin Ames

52279510R00092

Made in the USA
Lexington, KY
22 May 2016